O9-AID-732

MOMMY TIME

Sarah Arthur

90 Devotions
- for New Moms -

Mommy Time

SARAH
ARTHUR

Tyndale House Publishers, Inc.
Carol Stream, Illinois

Visit Tyndale online at www.tyndale.com.

TYNDALE and Tyndale's quill logo are registered trademarks of Tyndale House Publishers, Inc.

Mommy Time: 90 Devotions for New Moms

Designed by Jennifer Ghionzoli

Library of Congress Cataloging-in-Publication Data

Arthur, Sarah.
Mommy time : 90 devotions for new moms / Sarah Arthur.
pages cm
Includes bibliographical references and index.
ISBN 978-1-4143-7475-8 (hc)
1. Mothers—Religious life. 2. Motherhood—Religious aspects—Christianity.
3. Mothers—Prayers and devotions. I. Title.
BV4529.18.A78 2013
242'.6431—dc23 2012041003

Printed in the United States of America

21 20 19 18 17 16 15
8 7 6 5 4 3 2

For my mom, who made it look easy

CONTENTS

ACKNOWLEDGMENTS

MANY THANKS to Stephanie Rische, Katara Patton, Sarah Rubio, Kristin Kratky, and all the wonderful women who cheered me on in this project. Now we know the reason why there are few-to-no devotionals for new moms *by* new moms: attempting this is like climbing Mount Everest without supplemental oxygen. Thank you for helping me breathe.

To my supportive husband, generous parents, and understanding church family: you are the reason this book exists at all.

And to my son, Micah John, whose toddler mantra is "Why walk when you can run?": thank you for slowing down long enough for hugs.

CRAVING MOMMY TIME?

WELCOME TO THIS LITTLE devotional book of daily readings for new moms. Well, "daily" is probably a bit ambitious, so let's say "regular." Or more like "occasional." Okay, so you probably won't get to most of these devos till sometime next year, when your new baby has finally settled into a dependable nap routine and you've dug yourself out from under the pile of laundry that began before you went into labor. Trust me, I'm not offended. I'm a new mom.

If you're anything like me, you're craving Mommy Time. Time to yourself, time to breathe, time to actually finish a meal. The whirlwind of your child's first few days or weeks is over. Reality has set in: you're tired and overwhelmed. You know that carving out space for God every day is important; but so is, say, brushing your teeth—which itself has become a moving target. Life seems to demand that you pick one or the other, and tooth decay sounds expensive. So you put off prayer yet again.

While having a daily quiet time with God is a worthy

ideal, I'm deeply aware that motherhood is itself a spiritual discipline. And maybe that's the point. Maybe that's what this little book is about: cultivating awareness of God's presence in the small things, in the daily tasks of caring for infants. Finding joy in the details. Motherhood is a school of humility and self-sacrifice—if we open ourselves up to it—and those disciplines alone can bring us closer to the heart of Jesus.

So ditch the spiritual guilt. Take a breath. God is here, as close as your baby's heartbeat. Even if it's forty seconds, it's God's time, and he gives it to you freely. Yours. Mom's only. Mommy Time.

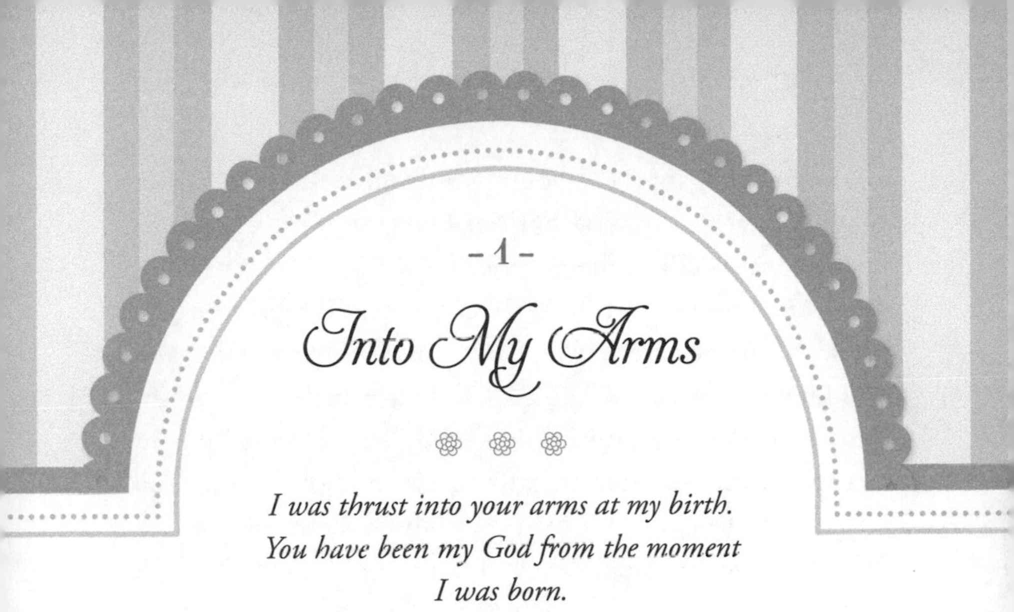

- 1 -

Into My Arms

I was thrust into your arms at my birth.
You have been my God from the moment
I was born.

PSALM 22:10

WELL, HE'S HERE. Our son has arrived. We didn't know he would be a *he* until my husband peered over the curtain of my unplanned C-section, paused for a moment, and then said hoarsely, "It's a boy?" (In the mess of emotions and bodily ick, he wasn't sure.) I was mostly delirious, so all I remember is a red, gooey, unhappy creature held out for me to see and my husband vanishing to hover over our new son while the baby was weighed and cleaned up. An angry squawk came from that direction—our son's first cry.

"It's okay, sweetheart," I croaked, even though I myself was totally unhinged.

Not a very illustrious beginning. But he's here. That's all we care about.

I won't go into the details of labor right now: everyone has their awful or amazing story. (Just hope my thirty-plus hours never happen to you.) We women enter the Labor Zone, aware of nothing but our bodies and the occasional annoyance ("What's that *beeping*? I don't care if it's someone's life support: turn it off!"). Time and other details seem to vanish into the haze of pain. Decisions are made, familiar and unfamiliar faces come and go, our bodies perform astonishing feats that we have not invented. The fleeting thought crosses our minds that we will never be normal again. And yet somehow none of it matters. Only the baby matters.

And now he's here. Pink and clean, wrapped in a blanket and sporting a striped hat that makes him look like a gnome. He blinks with unfocused eyes at the lights, the monitors, the figures coming and going, my looming face. All his movements are in slow motion, like he has found himself in a strange dream. Eventually the excitement wears off, we attempt a feeding, and then he sleeps, nestled against my neck, skin on skin.

After all this waiting, he has made his grand entrance, and I finally get to hold him in my arms. I get to inspect his comical face, his fringe of reddish hair (which looks like neither of his parents'), his little limbs and digits. Not many hours ago *all this* was inside of me. Totally surreal.

On his ankle he wears a tiny plastic band bearing our name, claiming him as ours, belonging to us. And yet, everything I know about my Christian faith tells me that this child is not really mine. As the Bible says in Psalm 22:10, the arms that *really* hold my child—the arms into which my child has been so unceremoniously shoved—are not mine, but God's. The one who created my son, the one who calls him into a life of faith, the one who gave up his own Son, Jesus—that's the one who truly holds him now.

Which is a good thing, because at present all I want to do is sleep.

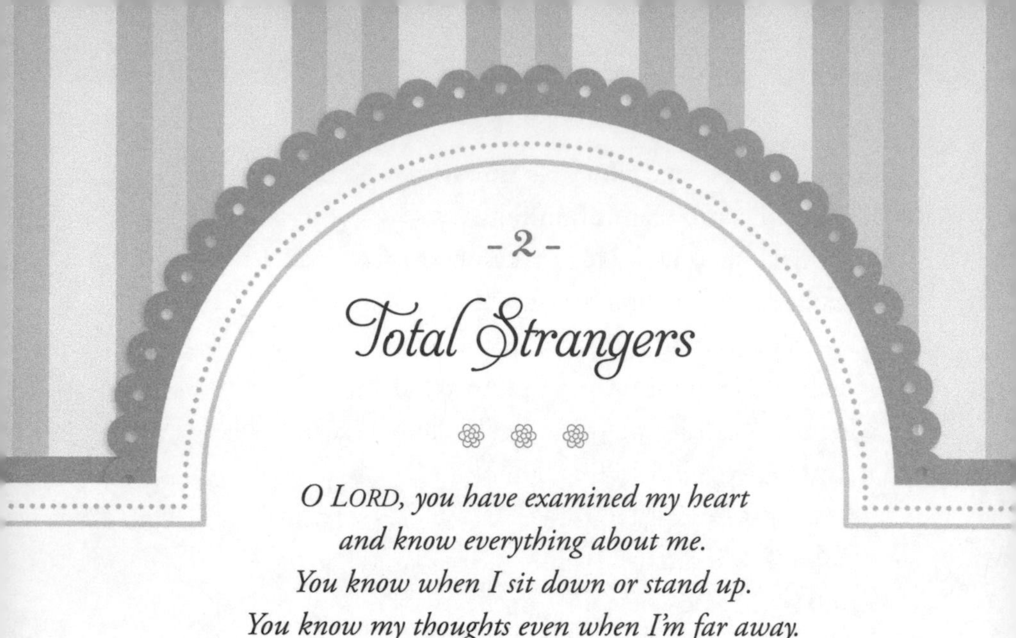

- 2 -

Total Strangers

O LORD, you have examined my heart
and know everything about me.
You know when I sit down or stand up.
You know my thoughts even when I'm far away.

PSALM 139:1-2

WHEN MY SON is handed to me for the first time, I feel the sudden dissonance of greeting a stranger I thought I knew before. It's like a blind date with someone you've only read about online. Nothing about his features is familiar, but then he'll make a move and I think, *Aha! That's just like him. That's the kick he used to give to my liver.*

On one level, it seems perfectly normal to have this little body that I've been carrying for nine months now sharing my personal space. In fact, handing him to someone else feels like cutting off my arm. Our post-op nurse (who happens to be a friend from church) has had to remind me that my parents might actually like to *hold* their new grandson. He has been part of me for so long that I can't yet grasp that he is now out there in the world.

On another level, he is clearly a distinct person, wholly

separate from me. He makes movements I don't anticipate and facial expressions that I've never seen before, and he has an overall alien look that makes me wonder what planet he came from. Snuggling him against my skin feels a little awkward, like necking with a complete stranger five minutes after we've met. I am the only world my child has ever known, but we are still a long way from really knowing each other. For that we have, God willing, a lifetime.

In the meantime I'm grateful that what is strange to me about my son—or about me to him—is not strange to God. Nothing about my character surprises my heavenly Father. He fashioned me, planned my steps, and knows my strengths and weaknesses better than I do. As Psalm 139:1 says, God has "examined my heart" and is aware of every movement I make, coming or going. My son may find my actions bewildering at times—it may take him years to figure out why I fly off the handle when he uses *that tone*—but God isn't baffled by any of it.

And likewise God knows my son inside and out. He knows the mysteries of this boy's personality, the paths he will choose (for better or worse), and the parts of his character that will bless and burden the rest of us. When my newborn moves beyond mere instinct and his brain starts to form coherent thoughts, God will know them all. When I stand in the kitchen, helpless, as my toddler babbles some incomprehensible description of an item he wants, God will know the deepest desires of my child's heart.

So I meet my son for the first time, and it's weird and wonderful. Thankfully, while we may be total strangers now, we both are known by the one whose knowledge matters most.

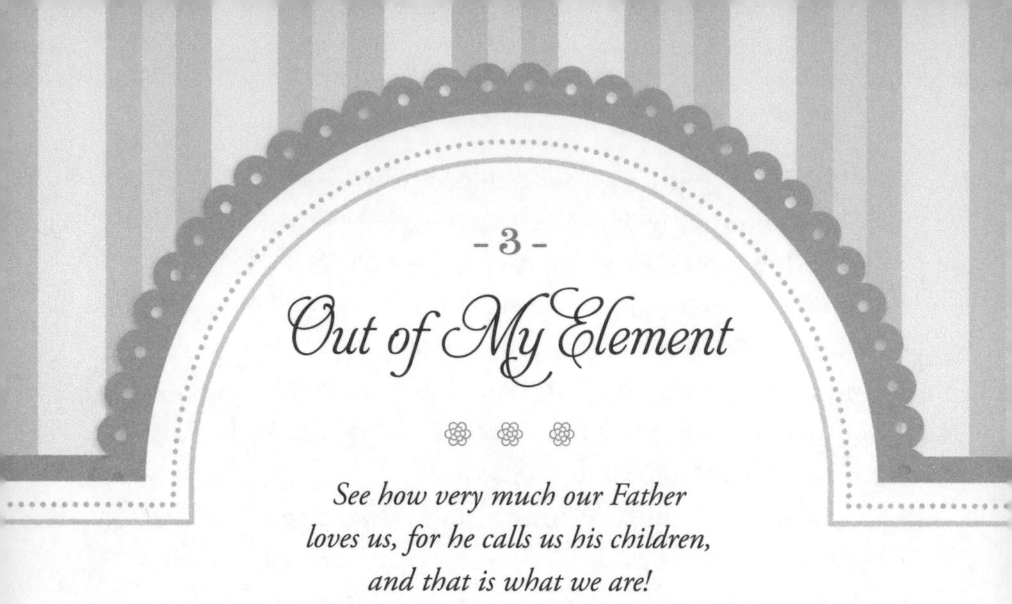

- 3 -

Out of My Element

See how very much our Father loves us, for he calls us his children, and that is what we are!

I JOHN 3:1

SO IT BEGINS. I AM NOW A MOTHER.

I don't know about you, but the thought both exhilarates and terrifies me. There's the thrill of entering a new stage in life, like traveling to India for the first time. I've been practicing the language, studying the guidebooks, rehearsing the stages of the journey so that I won't feel completely out of my element. I can't wait to get started.

But I *am* out of my element. That's instantly clear when the afternoon nurse asks, "When was his last feeding?" and I haven't the foggiest idea. Time? What does time have to do with anything? Oh, there's a feeding chart? Seems like an important thing to have noticed in the *huge* folder they gave me, the one I should have read through by now. I feel like I've landed in New Delhi, no one speaks my language, and the train I was supposed to catch just left the station.

Motherhood: it's a daunting prospect. I'm not particularly comforted by the fact that millions of women have done this before, in far worse circumstances, and thrived. All those legacies to live up to, all those overachievers who have given motherhood a good name . . . make me want to curl up in a ball and say, "Okay, would some expert please take over?"

It's a good thing my son doesn't care. I'm his mother—for life. If I find it thrilling, big deal. If I'm terrified, so what? All he knows is the warmth of my skin, which is warm enough for him; and the fact that we're *trying* to feed, which is better than not trying at all; and the rhythm of my voice, ragged with exhaustion, which he remembers from the womb and turns to like a flower to sunshine. We may still be adjusting to each other, but biology and God's providential oversight have at least determined our roles.

And maybe there's the comfort. Maybe that's where the courage comes from. Because I did not invent this whole parenting thing, I don't have to be the expert. That's God's forte—God the Father of Jesus from before time began; God the Father of Israel; God the Father of all who claim Jesus as Lord. As the writer of 1 John says, out of the Father's great love we have been claimed as God's children: "and that is what we are!" (1 John 3:1). He has been parenting us since before we were a thought in our earthly parents' heads, and he will do the same for our kids.

So I don't need to have this whole motherhood/parenting thing down. I can be out of my element for once. The expert, praise God, is already in the room.

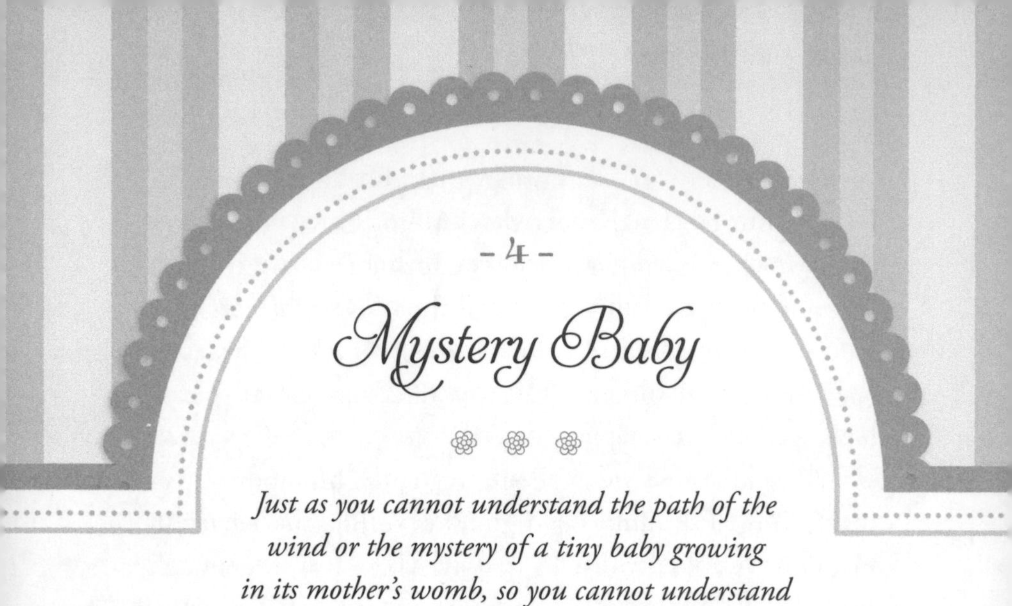

- 4 -

Mystery Baby

Just as you cannot understand the path of the wind or the mystery of a tiny baby growing in its mother's womb, so you cannot understand the activity of God, who does all things.

ECCLESIASTES 11:5

SOMEHOW WE HAVE SURVIVED the big event, that crazy thing called "having a baby." It lived large in my imagination for so many months, the inevitable, the unstoppable, the cataclysmic. Millions of women all over the world, since the beginning of creation, have done this; and yet during pregnancy I couldn't shake the unreasonable notion that I would be the one woman in the history of the planet whose body would not follow the usual pattern. I'd carry the baby for fourteen months, say, or we'd give birth to a giant egg, like a dinosaur. Or, on the flip side, I'd pop the baby out without even a groan, remarking, "What have all these gals been fussing about?"

But my body did exactly what it was supposed to do, even if Baby got stuck on the way and needed some help. Somehow my body knew what was required, what hormones to produce, what muscles to work, what ligaments to relax (all of them, it turns out: I feel like Gumby at the moment). I now know, in great detail, what the gals have been fussing about. Pause while I give a toast to the brave, the strong, the persevering, the valiant, the amazing mothers of the world.

The funny thing is, while I was there for the whole thing—the star witness, so to speak—I can honestly say I have no idea what happened. For months in advance I had watched video after video about pregnancy, labor, and delivery. I listened as aunties and grandmas shared their advice, including various predictions and proverbs about gender. But even after living through it, experiencing the event from the inside, I am no closer to understanding the great mystery of human life than I was before.

The entire process, from conception to delivery, may have all kinds of medical explanations; but in the end, do we really know what's going on? It's a mystery, as the writer of Ecclesiastes 11:5 says. Like the path of the wind, the way babies get here is unknown to us. And if all of that is mysterious, the great work of God is even more so.

The same God who manages the weather, stirs the wind, breathes across the face of the earth, is the same God who guided my small son into the world. And while as Christians we claim that God has fully revealed himself in Jesus Christ (see Colossians 1:15-20), he has not fully revealed *all* mysteries of the universe. For that we must wait till we see him face-to-face, and even then our minds may not be able to grasp the answers to all our questions.

How did our baby get here? Only God knows. But he's here, and that's what matters.

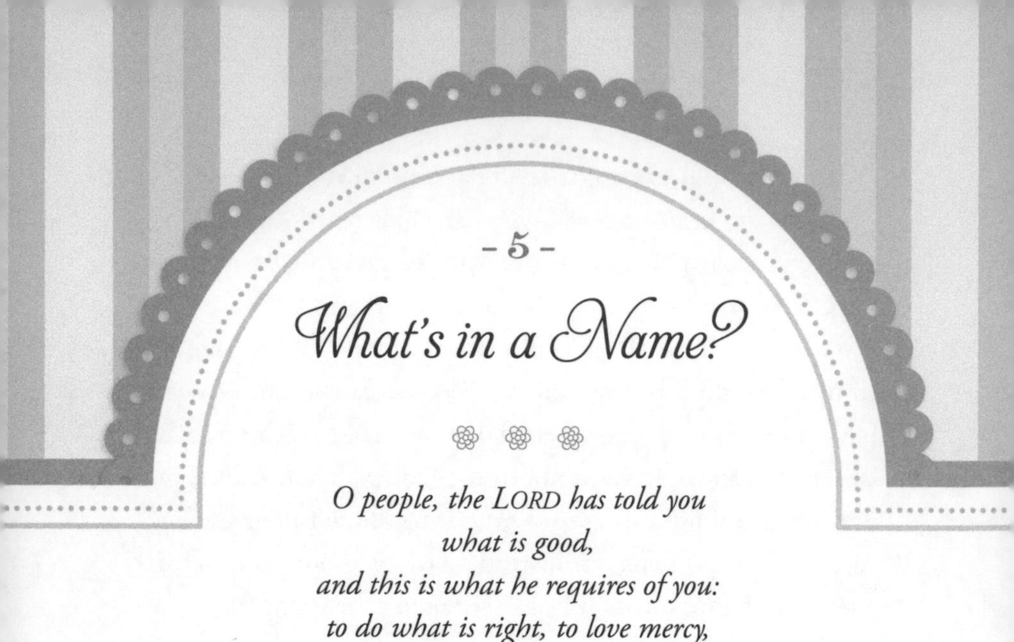

- 5 -

What's in a Name?

O people, the LORD has told you
what is good,
and this is what he requires of you:
to do what is right, to love mercy,
and to walk humbly with your God.

MICAH 6:8

AS I'VE ALREADY MENTIONED, my husband and I waited to know the gender of our baby until he arrived. We didn't have a deep theological reason for this; mostly we felt like the whole process of pregnancy was so clinical and medically monitored that it was nice to have at least one area of mystery. In the meantime we kept a secret short list of boy names and girl names, ready to bust out the top choice from the appropriate column when the time came.

Now our boy is here, and we have named him Micah John.

Most of our friends and family understand the "John" part—that's my husband's father. But the first name takes some explaining. Why not something a little easier, like Mark? Not that anyone's complaining: the overall reaction, even from total strangers, is positive. Micah? Oh, that's cool. But where'd it come from?

As you might guess from today's Scripture, the name Micah comes from an Old Testament prophet—a minor one, which is why a lot of folks haven't heard about him. The name itself is a variant of "Michael," meaning "Who is like Yahweh [God]?" It's meant to be a rhetorical question with only one right answer: no one. There is no one like God.

The prophet Micah lived during a time when God's people faced impending disaster. Long after King David, and long before the birth of Jesus, the nations of Israel and Judah had forgotten who God was. They worshiped other gods and oppressed the poor, blithely ignoring the threat of advancing armies from the north. Even after occasional spiritual revivals, the people did not turn fully away from their worship of idols. Prophets like Isaiah and Micah warned them, but it wasn't long before their capital cities began to fall.

What could the people do? Well, the prophet spells it out in Micah 6:8: do what is right, love mercy, and walk humbly with your God. In some translations, that command is not just for God's people but for all mortals: if you are breathing, this is for you. And it's not rocket science. It doesn't require a special degree or elaborate rituals or radical new politics. It's a way of life that any individual can strive for, whether one's surrounding kingdom falls or not.

So we have named our son after an obscure prophet from a tiny book of the Bible. And that's because we believe names mean something. They hold within them both a legacy and a calling. For Micah, the legacy is the story of God's people from centuries past, reminding us that no god can compare to ours. And the calling is the verse itself: simple, eloquent, memorable. If there's ever a moment in the future when Micah is unsure what to do, it's our prayer that he will run all options past the test of that passage.

Of course now the trick is, so should we. Because if we, his parents, can't live according to the requirements of that verse, why should we expect him to?

- 6 -

Heading Home

Don't be afraid; you are more valuable to God than a whole flock of sparrows.

MATTHEW 10:31

WE'RE BRINGING MICAH home from the hospital, and of course it's in the middle of a snowstorm during rush hour traffic. I sit in back next to the baby, leaning down periodically to make sure he's still breathing—because, you know, this is the first newborn in the history of the planet ever to ride in a car seat. All around us (I swear) are maniacs, chatting on their cell phones, one hand on the wheel, laughing, eating, *changing lanes*. I am certain we won't make it to the first stoplight.

After the entourage of medical professionals who surrounded us for five days in the hospital, where is the police escort, the motorcade, the respectful pulling over of traffic to let us pass? Am I just being unreasonable here, or does the fact that we are now the sole persons legally responsible for the care of a six-pound human being entitle us to something?

Apparently not. The planet goes on as usual, even though our little world is completely, unalterably changed. Babies are born every hour, every minute, every second, all around the globe; and meanwhile the sun still rises, the moon still sets, and people go on doing what they always do. There is no police escort announcing the arrival of The Most Important Thing Ever, no pedestrian saluting or flags unfurling or traffic being rerouted. My tiny son squirms in the car seat, his face crumpled and unhappy, rooting into the headrest whenever he hears my voice, just like the thousands of other brand-new babies around the world, coming home this very moment.

I know this in my head. I know God cares for each one of those little lives, those brand-new families. Jesus tells his disciples that their heavenly Father cares more about each one of them than for a whole flock of sparrows—and he cares for each sparrow enough to know when it falls (see Matthew 10:29). He has an interest in the safe arrival of every small person to the home that is waiting. If I were feeling creative, I could imagine protective angels defrosting an icy patch on the road ahead, or shielding us from the truck that's lost its brakes—and for all I know, that is what's happening. But all I see is how huge and dangerous and terrifying this planet is, how improbable that any newborn survives at all.

This is why God is God and I am not. Somehow he is able to be the Creator of the universe, casually bringing thousands of babies into the world by the day, at the same time that he is our loving Father, able to focus on this little human, right here, this one small person whose very existence depends on the vigilance of others. I take a breath, smile benignly at the driver in the next lane, and try to tell myself I will laugh about this later.

-7-

And Then There Were Three

What are mere mortals that you should think about them,
human beings that you should care for them?
PSALM 8:4

IS ANYONE ELSE STRUCK by the weirdness of going to the hospital as two people and coming home three people? When I had appendicitis, I didn't return from surgery with my appendix wrapped in a receiving blanket. But here we are, pulling into the garage and unloading the car as if we had just gone to the grocery store—where, apparently, there was a sale on babies.

For days afterward my husband or I say, "There's a baby over there" or "Where'd that baby come from?" and the other says, "That's crazy." My husband buys some balloons announcing "Baby" and ties them to the mailbox as if to say, "In case you didn't notice, our lives are radically changed forever!" We are not the first family on this block to tie baby balloons to a mailbox. I remember seeing one last summer, back when I was pregnant, and thinking, *Oh, that's so sweet,* as if they had just bought a new puppy. But it's a *human life*, small and vulnerable, a little personality that had not existed before. Does anyone else think how strange and impossible that is? Can I get an amen?

I stare at my son, his little body completely limp with one of those blissed-out sleeps that follows a good feeding, and I still can't grasp how one life could be at the same time so amazing and so ordinary. These fingers, so complex and beautiful, are the same design as every human finger around the globe. And yet they somehow came from my body, our bodies, not from anyone else's. This particular child, with his genetic makeup and temperament and the funny wrinkled *V* in his forehead, could not have happened in any other way.

Last week we were two, and now we are three.

And somehow it feels like my husband and I had very little to do with it. Sure, we showed up at the right moments and did our part, contributing our various genes and taking prenatal vitamins and pushing when the doctor said, "Push"(not that it did any good). But otherwise most of the process was veiled in mystery. There was nothing, and then there were bones and sinews and a heartbeat and the flutter of a kick.

Two became three. Who else but the God of the universe, who created the world *ex nihilo*, out of nothing, could do that kind of math? I'm like the psalmist who looked up at the stars and wondered how the Creator of all the vastness could still care for "mere mortals" (Psalm 8:4). The God who scattered galaxies across the universe and spun planets from particles is the same God who fashioned this small life from our small lives. Every once in a while I can almost hear him saying—with a mixture of proud daddy and bemused scientist—"Hey, there's a baby over there!"

- 8 -

So Much for the Dream

She gave birth to her first child, a son. She wrapped him snugly in strips of cloth and laid him in a manger, because there was no lodging available for them.

LUKE 2:7

OUR BABY WAS DUE December 15, which I envisioned as an appropriately festive time of year. I had dreams of coming home from the hospital to a house all decorated for Christmas, the smell of pine greeting us as we walked in. Holiday lights winking gently in the windows, soft candles burning on the mantel. And Christmas music, of course. The old favorites, the hymns and carols, and that album by Sarah McLachlan that always makes me cry.

I would rock my baby while humming "Silent Night." I'd trim the tree, hand decorate my homemade sugar cookies, then make a few phone calls to elderly shut-ins to wish them a Merry Christmas. All before whipping together an elaborate holiday dinner complete with traditional fixings, to which my extended family would sit down at the elegant table.

You know where this is going, right? Yeah.

By some divine joke, our baby has come three weeks early (more on that later), and whatever illusions I had about creating a haven of holiday peace have evaporated like snow in July. In a desperate attempt to reclaim the dream, this afternoon I turned on Sarah McLachlan before sitting down to nurse my son. The album was on repeat out of reach, and he took so long to eat that I was ready to throw a breast pump at the computer before it was all over. *If I hear "I'll Be Home for Christmas" one more time . . . !* So much for holiday cheer.

Reality has set in, my friends. Whatever peace-filled dreams we had about life after baby have been callously shoved aside. That line from "Silent Night," "all is calm, all is bright," elicits a caustic "Ha!" from my corner of the room. And to be honest, I wonder if it would have elicited a similar response from Mary, the mother of Jesus, herself.

I doubt she was thrilled to find out she had to give birth in a barn because there was no room anywhere else (see today's Scripture). Travel weary, bloody, exhausted, hungry, she very well could have gazed at the crowd of strangers staring at her child and thought, *What the . . . ? Get out of here!* Or even said out loud, "If you tell me about the angels one more time, I swear . . ." I can almost hear her muttering as she picks up Baby Jesus, "*Tender and mild*, yeah, right. Who came up with this stuff? And whatever happened to our hotel reservations?"

There's the dream, and then there's reality. And thankfully God isn't the author of the dream, so he helps us gently let it go. What we have in front of us is a gift. It may not be a silent night, but it is a holy one. And that's enough.

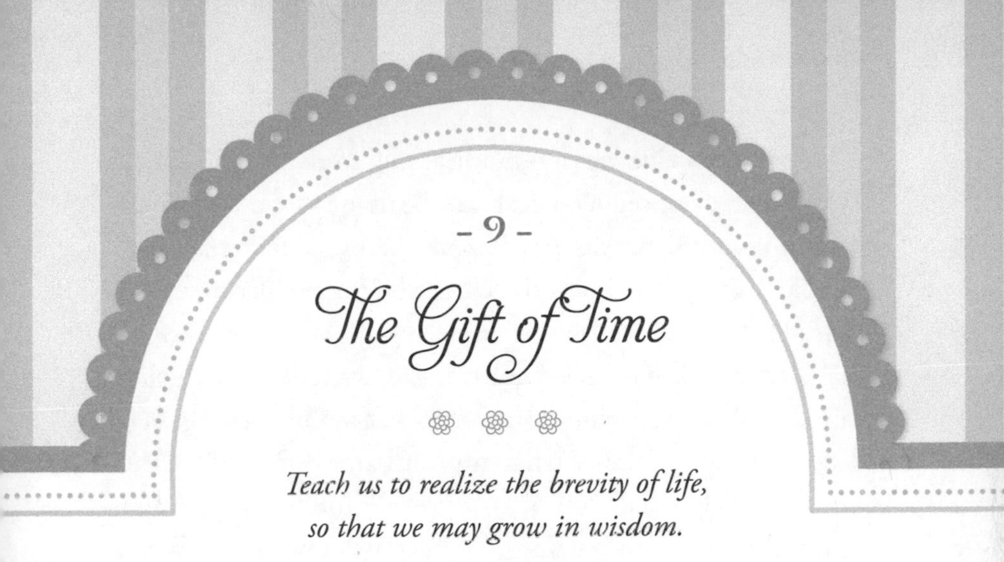

– 9 –

The Gift of Time

Teach us to realize the brevity of life,
so that we may grow in wisdom.
PSALM 90:12

IF HAVING TO STAY in the hospital for five days after my C-section wasn't bad enough (my son lost too much weight, so they wanted us to figure out the whole milk thing before I could leave), we have to turn right around and get him weighed at the clinic a few days later. So my husband, Tom, and I bundle him up and trudge out in the snow for the twenty-minute drive.

It's supposed to be a quick trip there and back, with a brief stop at Target on the way home. But no, it turns into an epic challenge worthy of *The Amazing Race*.

First, parking in the clinic garage is an exercise in both urban patience and physical endurance. We decide that Tom will drop me off at the door, where I'll wait while he parks and hauls in the car seat with the baby (I can't carry the car seat post-surgery). The closest spot must be a mile and a half away.

Then the weighing of our screaming son on a cold, hard metal scale is enough to tear my heart out—not to mention it involves two diaper changes, before and after. Since neither parent has gotten the hang of it yet, diapering takes a while.

After that it becomes clear our son wants to eat; so the nurse pulls the curtain, and the forty-five-minute feeding begins. I have no idea what my husband does the whole time: plays with his phone, maybe. I'm oblivious to anything else while I'm nursing, actually—yet another mystery of motherhood.

Then we traipse to another part of the clinic so Micah can have his blood drawn, for which my husband graciously says, "I'll take him." I don't think I can bear to hear my son wailing again. They return some time later, Micah red and unhappy, my husband grim. We make our complicated exit back to the parking garage, where (did I mention?) we are parked in the next state over.

On the ride home I am suddenly ravenous. Of course we haven't brought anything to eat, so we stop at a convenience store, and Tom bolts in for some PowerBars. Because I'm breastfeeding, he has to read all the ingredients to make sure there isn't any caffeine or weird substances—so by the time he returns I have almost started eating my seat belt.

If anyone is keeping track, we have been gone, by this point, for three hours.

And we haven't even stopped at Target yet.

I'll tell the rest of the story in the next devo, but in the meantime we've learned two very important things. First, always overestimate how long it takes to go anywhere with a newborn. And second, we may think we have all the time in the world, but as the psalmist says in Psalm 90:12, life is brief: time is a gift. It's not our job to pack the day full, but to do what's in front of us with grace. Easier said than done!

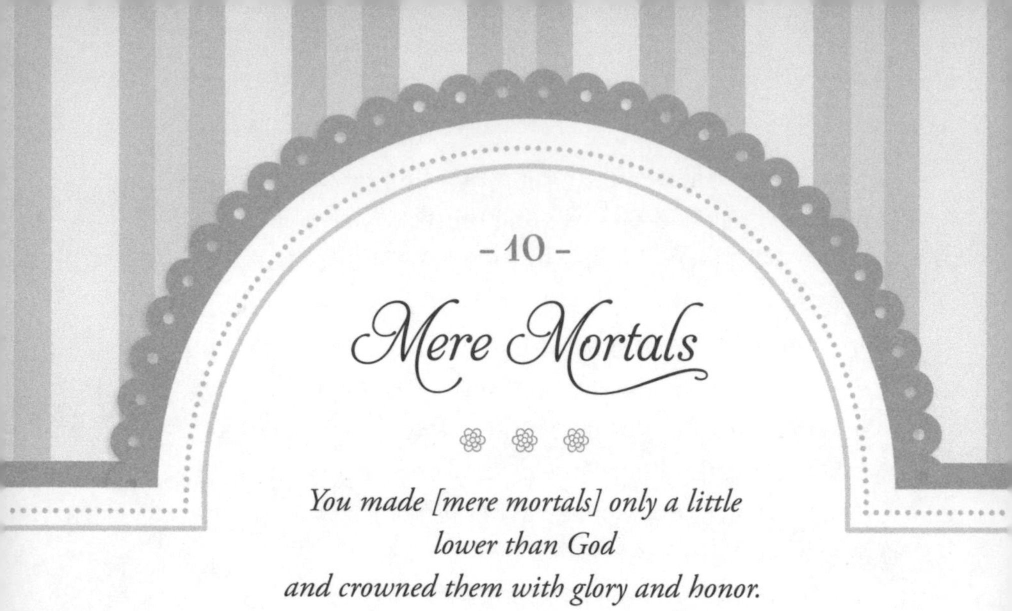

- 10 -

Mere Mortals

You made [mere mortals] only a little lower than God and crowned them with glory and honor.

PSALM 8:5

AS I DESCRIBED in the previous devo, "The Gift of Time," the supposedly quick trip to the clinic in order to weigh my seven-day-old son turned into what felt like a crazy episode of reality TV. Let's call this last leg the Target Debacle, for reasons that will soon become obvious.

By the time we trundle into Target, our last stop before home, I am exhausted. My husband, gently reminding me that I'm still recovering from major abdominal surgery, gets me an electric cart, which I proceed to maneuver at 0.003 miles per hour down the aisle—feeling, I might add, totally ridiculous. It doesn't help that we're there for the sole purpose of finding me a package of humongous granny underpants, which are the only type of panties I can wear over the incision from my C-section.

Tom carries the baby in the car seat, leading the way to the underwear section. There I park the cart, shuffle down a side aisle, and stand before the hopeless number of options. It must take me a while because when I return to the cart, Tom and the baby are gone.

"Tom?" I croak, looking around. No answer. I gingerly maneuver onto the cart and motor a few feet to look down the next aisle. Louder: "Tom?" No one. I put the cart in reverse, do an agonizing three-point turn, and head the other way. Still no Tom, no baby.

By this time my heart is pounding. What could have happened? There isn't a single other person to be seen. Have I missed a fire alarm? Is the baby in trouble? Unreasonable panic grips me. My breath comes in great gulps. I resist the urge—as strong as anything I've ever felt in my life—to let out a primal scream.

Instead I pick up my cell phone with shaking hands and call my husband. When his cheery voice answers, I begin to cry, managing to squeak out, "Where—are—you?"

He's there in an instant. "Right here, honey. See, the baby's right here." He holds out the car seat so I can see Micah, fast asleep. It's all I can do not to pick up the whole contraption and hug it. My husband caresses my hair, apologizes for stepping away—he had been hunting for something in the baby section, which was just one aisle over.

I'm emotionally undone. In a few short days I've gone from intelligent career woman to some sort of lower primate, all howls and grunts and basic biological functions. The change terrifies me.

I've already mentioned the psalmist's astonishment that God cares for "mere mortals" like us (see "And Then There Were Three"). But what really gets me is the phrase "You made them only a little lower than God"—or in some translations, "a little lower than the angels" (Psalm 8:5).[1] It's hard to believe, especially when I feel not much higher than a chimp in the cosmological hierarchy. But I suppose in this moment it's not what I think about myself, but what God thinks of me. When he made us, he not only thought we were good, but "very good" (Genesis 1:31). Postpartum hormones and all. And that's good enough.

– 11 –
Sleeping like a Baby

The one who watches over you will not slumber.
Indeed, he who watches over Israel
never slumbers or sleeps.

PSALM 121:3-4

IF THERE'S ONE THING I've learned about newborn sleep, it's that babies don't sleep like babies. They sleep like dinosaurs with really bad asthma. They sleep sounding like a sudden invasion of Bubble Wrap. My son in particular sleeps like he's conducting an orchestra while sprinting a marathon. If my hypervigilance wasn't enough to keep me up all night, the baby's own restlessness would. As I lie here in the semidarkness, watching his little jerks and twitches, I am jealous of whatever silent nights Mary the mother of Jesus supposedly enjoyed.

Meanwhile, my husband snoozes peacefully next to me in his hunting-orange earplugs—which is the only way we've figured out how to survive this whole newborn stage with one of us still sane. I shake Tom awake after I've finished a feeding, and he grunts and rolls out of bed to hang out with the baby until he (that is, the baby—though it's been known to happen to Tom, too) falls back asleep. And then we do it all again a few hours later.

Sleep. I miss it like an old friend.

When my body screams for rest, I find myself wondering how God does it. The psalmist assures us in Psalm 121:4 that God never gets tired, never snoozes on the job. Sure, God rested after creating the heavens and the earth (see Genesis 2:2). But the Bible doesn't say he slept. He merely took a break from the intense activity of creating the universe.

As the source of creation, God never walks away from it. He is never unconscious of it. He sustains it by his power, gives every atom its life and energy. He is, as the contemporary worship song says, the air we breathe.

And as far as we know, God hasn't rested since Genesis. Clearly this God is a different kind of parent altogether, a Super Dad of epic proportions. He is the ultimate sleepless parent, keeping vigil over creation and all of his people with unfailing attention. Even at three in the morning, as my husband and I finally drop with exhaustion next to our snuffling, snorting, tooting, wiggling newborn, God does not sleep. He is there, gazing at the child he has made, numbering every inhale and exhale like a new mom.

I can't sleep like a baby these days. But I can lift up a prayer of thanks to a God who keeps eternal watch over us all.

– 12 –
Hooked

Blessed are those who trust in the LORD
and have made the LORD their hope and confidence.

JEREMIAH 17:7

I'VE NEVER BEEN ONE for taking medication. Even though I've struggled with migraines for most of my adult life, I've usually hesitated to take anything till it's really, really bad. And of course, things wouldn't get really bad if I'd take something in the first place. But I'm cheap, and I don't want to become hooked on anything, and I don't always trust drug companies to have our best interests at heart.

But after my C-section, when the nurse in the hospital took one look at my ashen face and said, "You look like you could use some more painkillers," I replied, "Yes, please." If this wasn't what "really bad" felt like, I didn't want to know what was. So the regular regimen of painkillers began. Since we've come home I've dutifully kept track, on Micah's little feeding/pooping chart, of when and how much medication I've taken in a given day.

A few days ago I took a look at the chart and realized Micah had settled into a rhythm and was gaining weight, so we didn't need the chart anymore. Looking over the numbers, I was appalled at how much medication must be in my system. So I decided to cut that out too. I felt fine, so why was I pumping myself full of chemicals? It wasn't a well-thought-out plan, obviously. Just cap the bottle and put everything away. I'm great.

Yeah, well, I'm paying for it now. This morning I sank into the couch, gripped by a headache worse than I've felt in months. I couldn't understand it: why was I so ill? Was I doomed to have migraines again, forever and ever, my son's only memories of me as a pale, supine figure on the couch, eyes covered by a washcloth?

"Did you take anything for it?" my husband asked. There was a pause.

"Oh," I replied, my brain suddenly catching up with my body. Of course. It wasn't a migraine: I was simply detoxing. I had become addicted, in a few short weeks, to painkillers. Moms, apparently, can get hooked on drugs.

So the regimen has begun again, and the headache has vanished. But now I'm ready: I'm cutting pills in half, prepared to slowly wean myself off painkillers till my body can handle doing life on its own again. I'm determined to not renew my prescription.

It's a strange experience, not trusting yourself. I learned to trust my body all throughout pregnancy—even during labor and delivery—when my body seemed to know what it was doing. Even when my brain couldn't anticipate the genius things my body could perform—ah, milk, at just the right moment!—I knew to relax and let my body handle it. But now the situation is reversed. My body is the one that has betrayed me. If the human heart is deceitful, as Jeremiah 17:9 says, the human body is no saint either. That's why Jeremiah reminds us, in verse 7, to put our trust in God alone.

- 13 -
Crying Out

In my distress I cried out to the LORD;
yes, I cried to my God for help.
He heard me from his sanctuary;
my cry reached his ears.

2 SAMUEL 22:7

OUR SON HAS FINALLY learned how to cry. This may sound baffling to those who had full-term babies with lungs like opera singers, but to those with late-preterm babies, you know what I mean. Born three weeks early—and probably doped up on all the pain medication I've had to take after my C-section—he has mostly just wanted to sleep all the time. I've actually had to set my alarm every three hours in order to wake him up for feedings.

If I could find a Onesie that summarizes my son's basic philosophy so far, it would say, "I'd Rather Be Gestating."

During these first few weeks his grandmothers have commented with astonishment on how "good" he is, meaning he never cries. Warm and snuggly, occasionally rooting around, he's been the ultimate dream baby.

Well, all I can say is, "Stick around, ladies. The fun has just begun."

Forget the alarm: Micah will now tell me in no uncertain terms that his belly is empty. He has been forsaken, the world is coming to an end, I am the worst mother in the world. He knows how to get my attention: screw up the face, suck in a mighty lungful, and let it rip. Sometimes it seems like he's holding a contest to see if he can make himself turn redder (or even bluer!) than last time. I'm beginning to miss the alarm.

The good news is, Micah is growing. He is learning to communicate. He is using the only technique he knows to get our attention, and he has discovered that it works. *Loud noises come from my mouth, and Milk Lady responds? Cool. Let's try that again. Ooh, there she is! Louder. Let her know I'm mad. That's right. Where's the milk?*

As we settle in for a feeding, I am newly aware of God's own responsiveness to us. All throughout Scripture God's people cry out to him for help, for nourishment, for grace. Like newborns, they seem perfectly comfortable telling God exactly what they need, when they need it, and how it makes them feel when they don't get it. One of the greatest songwriters of all time, King David of Israel, tells how he cried out to God, and God responded (see today's Scripture). It's a biblical pattern: call and response.

And that's the thing: God responds. Otherwise humans would not have gotten in the habit of calling upon him, millennium after millennium. Just as Micah has learned that I will appear sooner or later once he starts wailing, the people of God have developed strong spiritual lungs. God may not always respond instantly, or with the answer that we desire, but he hears us.

So why do I hesitate in crying out to him?

- 14 -

Relentless

Have you never heard?
Have you never understood?
The LORD is the everlasting God,
the Creator of all the earth.
He never grows weak or weary.
No one can measure the depths of his understanding.

ISAIAH 40:28

SOMEONE ASKED ME yesterday how motherhood was going, and I said, "It's relentless." I'm not sure what I was expecting, but it just never stops. The sun rises and sets and I never get to take a lunch hour or a coffee break or even a quick dash to the bathroom. I have mastered the art of doing everything one-handed, baby in the crook of my arm. I am not ashamed to admit that I have successfully peed without dropping my child.

And meanwhile, once he's napping, I regularly ignore the sage advice to sleep while the baby sleeps. Instead I run around trying to feed myself or throw yet another load of laundry in the wash. (How *does* such a small creature generate so much mess?)

Motherhood never stops. It just ramps up a level, and then another. It's like a treadmill. It's like living with a personal marathon trainer. It's like a master's degree program in which you're always cramming for exams and there's no graduation. Okay, so there are high points, too, but at the moment I'm overwhelmed.

My son's needs are relentless; but, I suppose, so are mine. And God never stops meeting them. He has never failed to give me breath in the morning. He has never failed to fill my belly, shelter my body, pour out the abundance of his grace through my loving family, friends, and fellow Christians. If my needs are relentless, then so is his love.

The prophet Isaiah gets at God's relentlessness when he asks, "Have you never heard? Have you never understood? The LORD . . . never grows weak or weary" (Isaiah 40:28). When faced with the unflagging needs of an unflaggingly needy world, God doesn't collapse at the end of the day, completely spent. He doesn't grumble when—just as he's settling down with a cup of Darjeeling and a good novel—yet another prayer request comes his way (okay, so God probably doesn't drink tea or read novels, but you know what I mean). His arm never grows weary of holding us, even as he busily brings down kings or reconciles sisters.

And that astounds me. That's the kind of God I want to worship. That's the kind of God I want my baby to know someday. Even when Micah himself grows weary, when he feels overwhelmed with work or ministry or parenting, I pray that he will put his hope in the God whose relentless strength never fails.

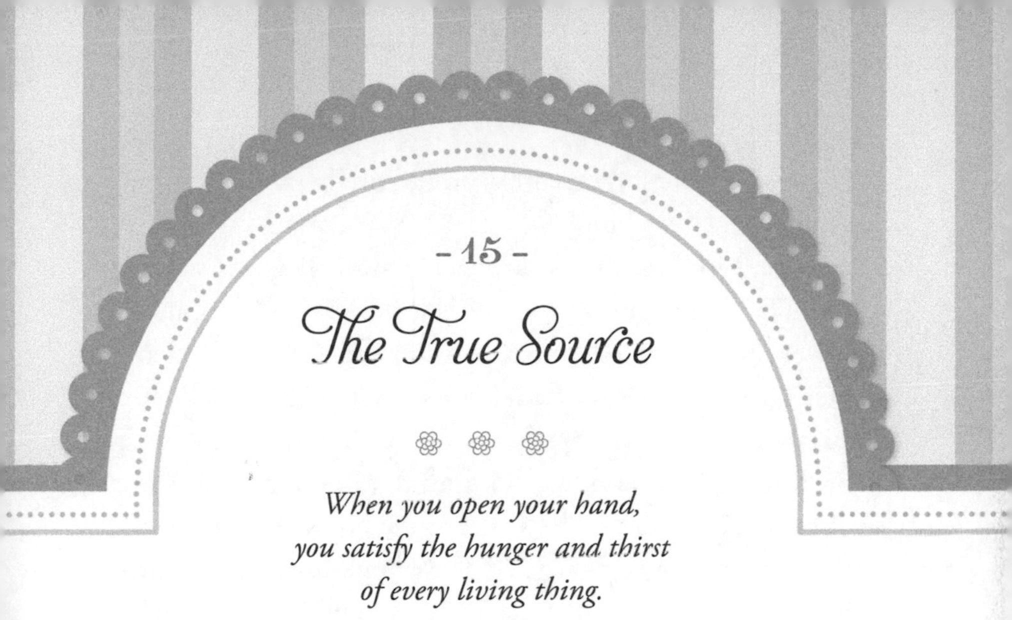

– 15 –

The True Source

When you open your hand,
you satisfy the hunger and thirst
of every living thing.

PSALM 145:16

EVER SINCE I WAS A CHILD my family has said a mealtime prayer based on the King James Version of Psalm 145:15-16:

The eyes of all wait upon thee, O Lord.
Thou givest them their meat in due season.
Thou openest thine hand, and satisfiest the desire
of every living thing.

Yes, that last line was a bit tricky, especially once I got braces. But I understood the point. Even as we sat down to eat the food my parents had worked for, my parents made clear that they weren't the source of it. Sure, all eyes turned to Mom as she brought a plate of meat from the oven to the table. And we knew she had prepared it because she loved us and wanted us to live healthy, productive lives. But the true source was God.

I have to remember that when my small son is wailing to be fed. I drag myself out of bed in a haze of sleepiness, wavering between relief that he's still breathing and resentment that he needs me so relentlessly. Staying in bed is not an option: my whole body responds to his cries with needs of my own. The need to hold him, to calm him, to get him to stop fussing, to feed him. I can't *not* take care of my son.

The amazing thing is, God doesn't take care of us because he needs to. He's not like me, the parent of a newborn, who is burdened by personal responsibility, hormones, and the laws of society to care for this child. And likewise he doesn't do it because we're just so darn lovable. I can't help picking my child up when he cries—not because I'm so great at this whole parenting thing but because he is so fabulously cute when he wrinkles his nose like that. Not so with God: if his care of us were based on our inherent lovableness, we'd all be in deep trouble—because, let's be honest, there's a lot about us that's hard to love, as our kids will find out soon enough.

No, none of these things motivate our God in his relentless care of us. Rather, he loves because love is at the heart of his character (see 1 John 4:8). That's the true source of his sustaining power. He chooses freely, out of the deep well of his love, to uphold the whole world. God loves us—not because of some deep biological need or our inherent lovableness—but because God *is* love. Any other response would be, in every sense of the phrase, out of character.

Someday, when my son is bigger, I'll tell him the same thing my parents told me: I may have provided these things for you, but God is the true source. So openest thine hand, buster. You're about to be satisfiest.

- 16 -

The Wisdom of Humility

Pride leads to disgrace,
but with humility comes wisdom.

PROVERBS 11:2

WE'VE FINALLY FIGURED OUT a strategy for calming Micah down, which is to pass him off to his father. Tom, bless his manly body, lacks the necessary apparatus for sending Micah into a frenzy of blind groping and wailing. Something about that uncompromising male chest and those firm arms signal "Chill out, dude" in ways I never can.

Tom also has become a master at what one leading pediatrician has called the five Ss: swaddling, swinging, side-lying, sucking, and shushing.[1] But Tom has added a sixth *S*: shock and awe. In short, Micah is swung in his car seat like he's on a Tilt-A-Whirl while the vacuum cleaner runs at top volume a few inches away. Magic.

Of course, this is the strategy that works today, or this hour. By evening we will have resorted to something different. Exhibit A: My husband is now fiddling with an old radio, attempting to find a fuzzy non-station that will generate white noise for Micah's room so we don't have to buy one of those expensive gadgets. He has already figured out that we can download the sounds of ocean waves and rainfall from the Internet: now comes the trick of rigging up a set of speakers in the right locations. We're cheap, but we're creative, by golly.

Parenthood, we've come to realize, is an exercise in improvisation. What works one day may not work the next. Every child is different. Experts swear by their various approaches to infant eating, sleeping, soothing, and diapering; but for every list of five Ss there's an alternative list suggesting just the opposite or claiming a superior source. If we're not careful, we could spend our son's infancy putting him through a regimen of tricks devised by outside experts rather than relying on the skills and wisdom God has already given us.

We may not have been trained in parenting so far, but we have learned, over time, how to read another human being. We have learned, for instance, that touch is vital to human flourishing, that encouragement and affirmation are keys to learning, that people get crabby when they're hungry or tired (grown-ups just don't cry about it—well, most of us, anyway). And sometimes people are crabby for no reason at all. This kind of wisdom we can bring to bear on the art of parenting, knowing that we may have to improvise, making tweaks and adjustments along the way.

It's a wisdom forged in humility, as Proverbs 11:2 says. If I were so set on being the know-all mother who can calm her child better than anyone else, I would not pass off my son to his father, who has the magic touch after all. If we were so set in using a certain parenting technique, believing that it—and our parenting—is the best, then we never would discover the hundred other things that work. Parenting is humbling stuff. But in the end, I pray, it leads to even greater wisdom than we have now.

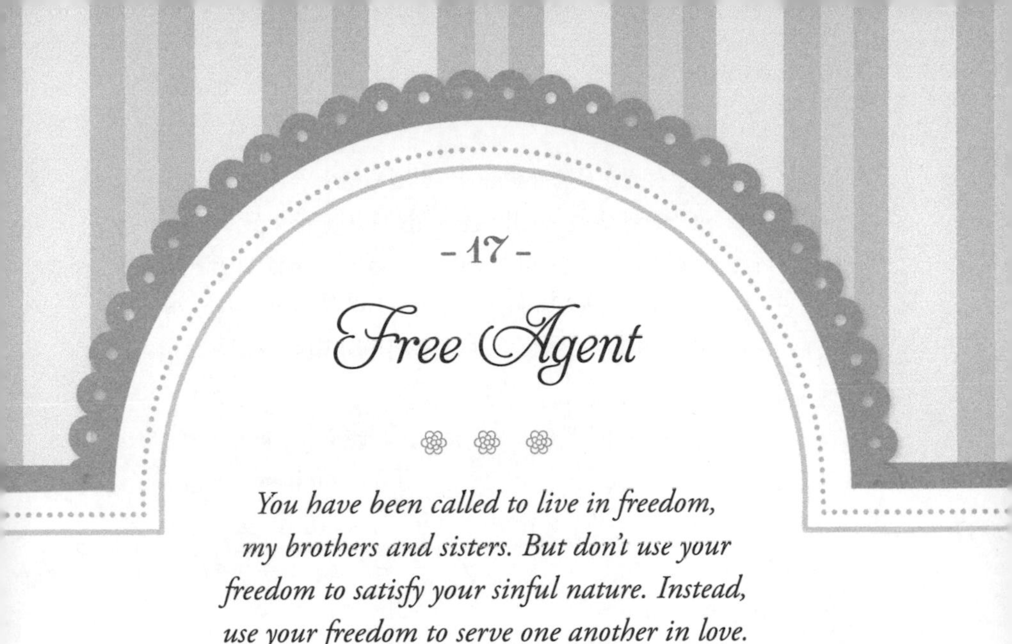

– 17 –

Free Agent

You have been called to live in freedom, my brothers and sisters. But don't use your freedom to satisfy your sinful nature. Instead, use your freedom to serve one another in love.

GALATIANS 5:13

SO I'VE HAD MY first baby dream—well, my first since Micah was born, anyway. I'd had dreams before, when I was pregnant—dreams that I delivered a girl, or that I had forgotten to tell my parents and then realized after a few days, "Oh, yeah, they should probably know I had a baby," and so forth. But this was my first postdelivery Micah dream.

I wouldn't call it a nightmare, although it did leave my heart pounding. The plot was a bit muddy at first: I was out and about, maybe shopping, or roaming a festival of some kind, indulging my freedom. But suddenly it hit me: I was a mother. I was in charge of a baby. And I had no idea what I had done with him.

I started running. There was a blur of city streets and then a large rambling church building, and I found myself vaulting up some sort of winding staircase two steps at a time. At the top I burst into a nursery full of babies and volunteer caregivers, relieved to see my son in the arms of a woman who looked relatively harmless, if a bit flustered. And instead of saying, "I'm so sorry! I can't believe I just left my son here without even telling you his name!" I simply said, "Did he cry the whole time?"

The dream went blurry again when I took my son and tried to make a quick, embarrassed exit. That's when I woke up and rolled over to make sure that Micah was still here, snoozing peacefully in the bassinet by the bed. I put my hand on his warm torso, feeling the rise and fall of his tiny chest. "I'm right here, baby," I said—which, at the moment, felt like a shady attempt to pretend nothing criminal had just happened. I haven't been able to shake the sense of guilt all day.

It's a bit annoying, actually. I mean, we mothers feel guilty enough without having to feel shame for something we only dreamed about! But it is a vivid reminder that I am not the person I used to be, able to make my way in the world without much of a care for anyone else. Sure, I kept my husband informed about my movements so he could plan his day, and occasionally I called my parents to check in, but otherwise I was a free agent. For a long time.

It's a hard transition. It's a step in maturity, even in spiritual maturity. While in Christ we are promised freedom—from sin, from bondage to our "sinful nature," as it says in Galatians 5:13—it's not freedom to do whatever we want. It's freedom to love and serve others. If motherhood doesn't force me to mature in this area of my life, I don't know what will!

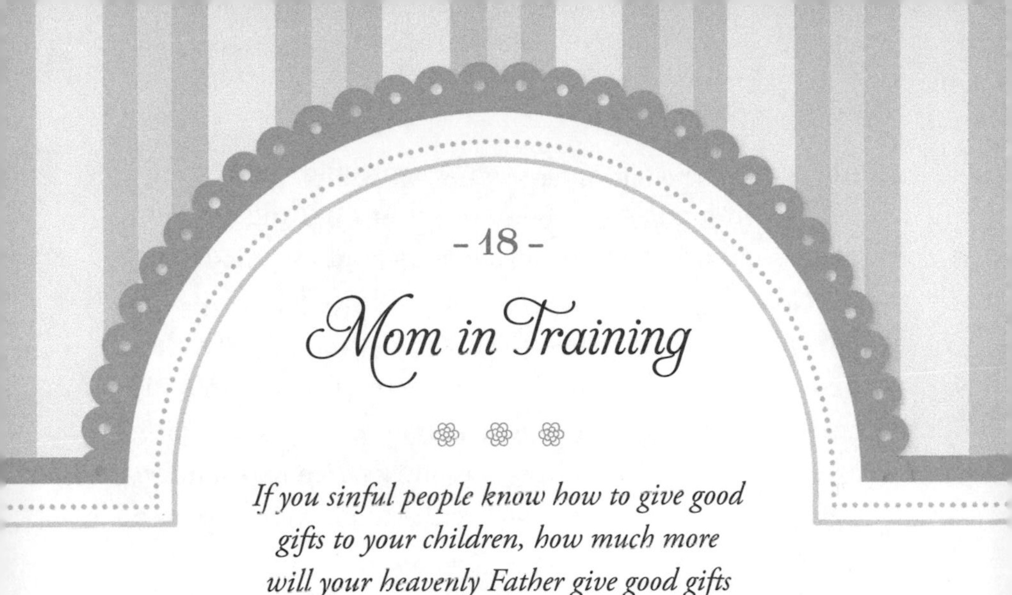

-18-

Mom in Training

If you sinful people know how to give good gifts to your children, how much more will your heavenly Father give good gifts to those who ask him.

MATTHEW 7:11

I'VE COME TO CHURCH today wearing the only clean shirt I have, which is a silly nursing top that I bought in desperation last week. I couldn't find anything else at the maternity store in my size (that I could afford), so I ended up with a hoodie meant to look like an athletic top that says, "Mom in Training." Several women from my small group approach, grinning.

"Love the top," one of them remarks.

"When do you stop being a mom in training?" another asks.

"Never," says an older lady with grown children.

"Does Micah have a matching one that says, 'Baby in Training'?" someone else asks.

"No," I say. "I wish."

"Are you kidding?" another new mom says. "You can't train a newborn."

"So much for a parent-centered household, huh, Sarah?"

And on it goes. For the record, I was not the one who used the phrase "parent-centered household" to describe my anticipated parenting style (although I have been known to say, back when I was child free, that if I ever had kids, they would *not* act like *that*). Parent centered has not been the goal of the Arthur household: we recognize that each new addition to our family changes it, just as each new number changes an equation. But neither has child centered been our plan.

Life with a newborn is a give-and-take kind of thing. I'm learning, and Micah is learning, and my husband is learning. Even our parents are learning. Micah gets his way some of the time: he has figured out, for instance, that if he cries someone will eventually pick him up. But I, his mother, also get my way some of the time: Micah does not get to choose whether or not he wants a diaper change. He can be as unhappy as he wants; the diaper will be changed. Win some, lose some, but no one gets to be the center all the time.

Sometimes I wonder how God manages the whole parenting thing. If there's anyone who deserves to be the center, who has the power and wisdom to know what's best for all creation, it's the one who made it. If there is a parent-centered setup anywhere, it would be the universe in which God is Lord and King. And while on one level that is the case—the universe is not a democracy—on another level God is unfathomably generous to his children, sharing his power with us all the time. He gives us the free will to make our own choices; he honors the rhythm of our human bodies; he even, as today's Scripture says, answers our prayers.

He is not a parent in training, but neither is he a dictator. Out of his great love he responds when we express our unique needs and desires. That's the kind of parent I'm training to be.

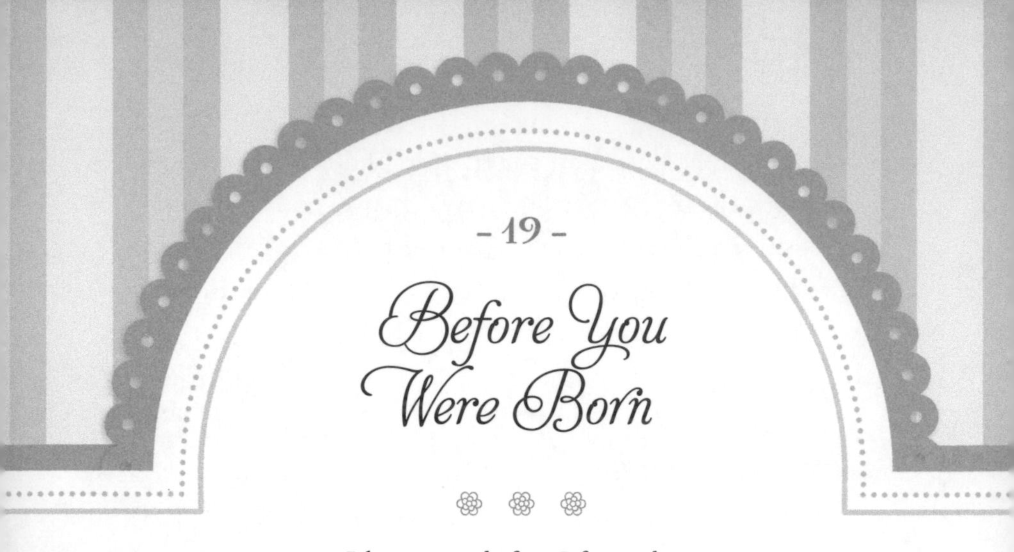

– 19 –
Before You Were Born

I knew you before I formed you
in your mother's womb.

JEREMIAH 1:5

WE TOLD OUR PARENTS that we were pregnant on Mother's Day. After well over a decade of waiting and then giving up on us, they were uniformly astonished. My mother-in-law, instead of saying, "Oh, congratulations! When are you due?" burst out with, "What changed your mind?" As if our minds were the only things involved.

We all laugh about it now, but there was a kind of general shock that hasn't died down even since the baby was born. And it extends to Tom and myself. After thirteen years of child-free marriage—with the exception of about three years in a community house full of kids—we are now more than just a couple. We are a family. Holy cow.

So what changed our minds? Mom's question was a good one, actually. Because for many years, whenever anyone would ask if we were planning to have a family, we would say, "Oh, maybe. But we don't sense we're supposed to do that right now." Our minds really were the key players. But then we finished graduate school, Tom became a pastor, and we settled into a new life. And both of us, on our own, began to wonder if maybe God wanted us to at least start *thinking* about family.

My body wasn't getting any younger, for one thing. And we now lived halfway between our two families, for another. And meanwhile Tom was preaching week after week to parents and families without having any inside experience of what parenting is like. Plus, there was that little command in Genesis 1:28 about being fruitful and multiplying—which, as far as we knew, had never been revoked. So we began talking about it, relieved to hear that the other spouse had been thinking about it too. Then one morning in January, Tom emerged from the shower, threw on his clothes, and came out to where I was standing in the kitchen.

"I think I'm ready," he said.

"Ready for what?"

"Well, not really ready," he corrected himself. "I think we're supposed to do this."

"Do what?"

"Try having a family."

"Oh! Okay." Pause. "Like, right now?"

He grinned. "Well, right now I have to go to work. But soon. Whenever you're ready."

"Okay. Wow. Um, sure."

So I talked with my doctor, and she gave us a game plan, and by April 1 we were pregnant.

I know it doesn't happen this way for everyone—a clear sense of God's prompting and then getting pregnant on the first try. That just happens to be our story. But, as I look back on it, I don't think that what God had in mind was some vague, generic idea of "family." I think what he had in mind was Micah. Like the prophet Jeremiah in today's Scripture, my son was known by God before he was even conceived, just as God has known every person in the world, every baby conceived this hour.

When my husband and I sensed that it was time, it wasn't just time for family in general but for this specific boy, crashed out in the cradle over there, a sleep grin suddenly crossing his face. What we thought was a gentle prompting was a person, waiting to be born.

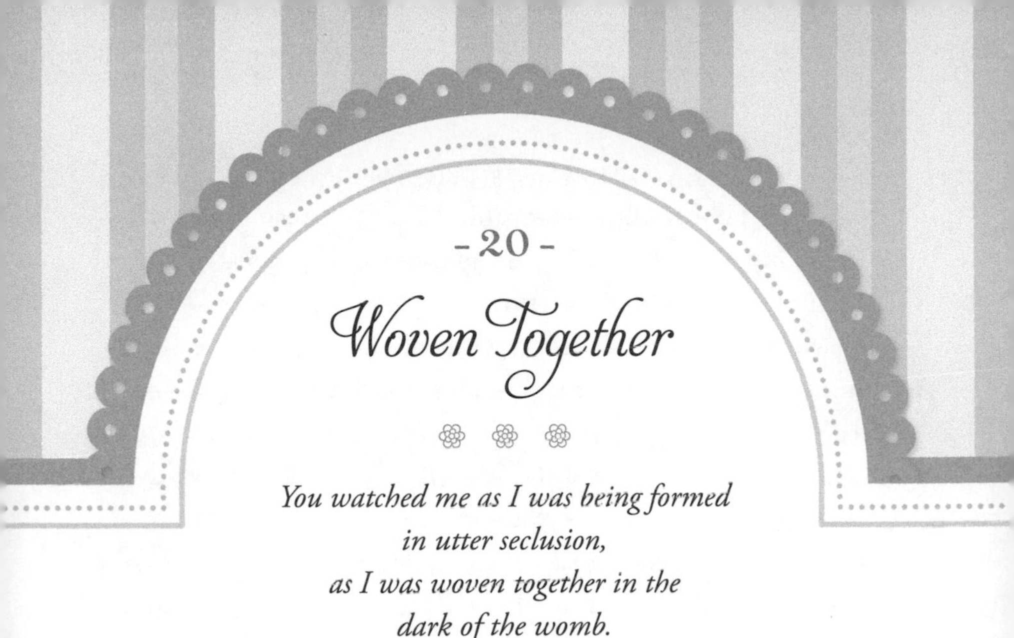

- 20 -

Woven Together

You watched me as I was being formed
in utter seclusion,
as I was woven together in the
dark of the womb.

PSALM 139:15

PSALM 139 HAS ALWAYS been one of my favorites. The psalmist's reassurance that God knows and cares about the intimate details of our lives—from before we were conceived to the last breath we take—has been a lifeline whenever I've wondered if God is actually paying attention. As the psalm describes, not only is God paying attention, but he is guiding and guarding, leading and upholding every breath, every step, every day of my life. We are held in the arms of one who knows us better than we know ourselves.

Throughout our marriage my husband and I have maintained a fairly regular pattern of prayer. That's mostly been blown to pieces lately (as I'll describe in some upcoming devos), but part of the pattern includes reading a psalm together, one person taking the odd verses and the other, the even verses. One evening partway through my pregnancy it happened to be Psalm 139. With each verse of mine, my voice became more and more wobbly until finally I couldn't read anymore. Tom asked, "Are you okay?"

Now, my husband has a wonderful heart, but he will freely admit that he doesn't always get it. He had read Psalm 139 that same morning—had even memorized it at one point in his life—but didn't experience it any differently this time around than he had before we got pregnant. I, on the other hand, was a sappy mess. Here was this beloved passage, which I had read all my life and knew so well, suddenly coming alive in a way that I had never heard it before. As the baby turned and kicked and wiggled inside of me, I was struck anew by the gentle reassurance that God was in charge of every aspect of this child's life before he or she ever took a breath.

Sure, it was my body that was doing the work, so to speak. I was the one who generated an entirely new organ and developed an entirely new human being, all in the space of a few months. I was the one climbing up the stairs, short of breath, or eating the entire contents of the refrigerator in one sitting. But as intimately as I know my own body, I didn't know the deepest mysteries of what was going on in there. The hidden personality of the little human inside of me, whose character will emerge over time like the unfolding of a flower, was already known fully by only one Person: God.

I failed to articulate this to Tom in the moment: all I could do was cry those sad-happy tears that bewilder men around the world and babble something about hearing the psalm again for the first time. He came over and held me and put his hand on my belly, and we laughed at my sappiness and his cluelessness. And we knew we would never read Psalm 139 the same way again.

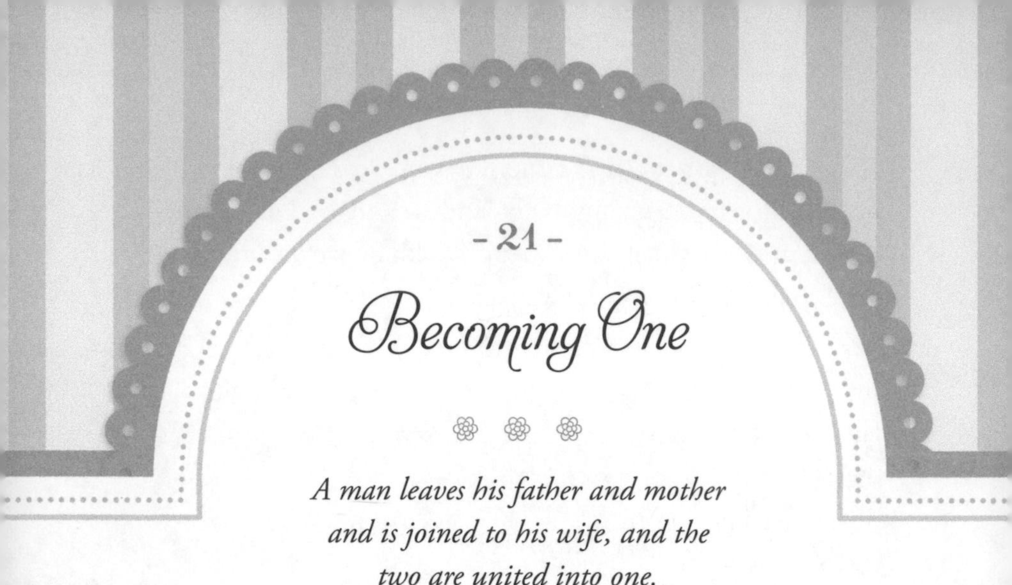

- 21 -

Becoming One

A man leaves his father and mother and is joined to his wife, and the two are united into one.

GENESIS 2:24

SO WE'RE A FAMILY NOW. It takes some getting used to. I wish the adjustments could happen overnight, but who am I fooling? When we were first married, it took us about two years of getting used to each other, of meshing our lives into one household, before we began to hit our stride. If marriage has taken that long, what about parenthood?

In fact, my husband and I are still learning how to be a couple, after fourteen years. We had been married eight years before we ever flew on a plane together. As we buckled in for an overseas flight, I looked at my husband and thought, *I wonder what he's like on a plane? Does it make him nervous? Does he read or sleep or talk to the people next to him? Does turbulence make him sick?* This person that I thought I knew so well had suddenly become a stranger again, like I had just met him in the waiting area and found out we were seated next to each other. Good thing he was cute. Really cute.

And then I think it was last summer that I heard my husband get the hiccups for the first time. They were unlike any other hiccups I had ever witnessed; and rather than being sympathetic or offering suggestions for getting rid of them, I laughed hysterically. "Thanks, honey," he said. We had been married more than a dozen years, but until that moment we hadn't known that (a) Tom's hiccups are rare and violent; (b) Sarah finds this hilarious; and (c) she is of no help whatsoever.

The learning is ongoing, and I imagine it will continue long into old age. My husband will develop a sudden interest in Indian cooking, perhaps; or I'll announce, out of the blue, that I'm entering a bike race. We will continue to surprise, challenge, and entertain each other. The project of becoming "one," as today's Scripture says, is more than just a spiritual reality: it is an ongoing process that involves leaving the family of origin, joining to the new spouse, and becoming unified over time.

If this is true with marriage, then adding a third person to the picture is yet another exercise in making adjustments, learning to accommodate, making compromises. As I mentioned in earlier devos, it will take some time to get to know this little person, even though his character is intimately bound to our combined DNA and to the household in which we raise him. It will take us a while to become a family.

But it won't be a forever thing: one day he will leave us

and, most likely—although God may have other plans—join with someone from yet another family, and the whole process of "oneing" will begin all over again. Hopefully by then he will have learned, by observing our family, that the process is not instantaneous but a gradual growing in grace.

- 22 -

Not My Own

For you, a thousand years are as a passing day,
as brief as a few night hours.

PSALM 90:4

IT HAPPENED INSTANTANEOUSLY, the moment I went into labor: one day my husband and I were happily following the usual pattern of our daily schedule, and the next day that schedule was totally—perhaps permanently—annihilated.

We have been married long enough that we had settled into a fairly consistent pattern, largely shaped by our work in the church. Monastic quiet in the mornings, work all day, quick dinners together, meetings in the evenings, Fridays off, date night, work on Saturdays, and crazy Sunday mornings followed by long afternoon naps. Despite moving seven times in four years during graduate school and living for a while in an intentional Christian community, we had managed to maintain that pattern overall.

Until now. Enter squalling infant at 2 a.m. Diaper blowout just as we're headed to church. Lunch at 4 p.m., dinner at . . . oh, forget dinner. Day off? Never heard of it.

We can sustain this new nonpattern for only so long before we start to unravel. Okay, so we can only sustain it for about four days. That's where the grandmas and grandpas come in—and our amazing church family, which keeps us supplied with meals for nearly two weeks. But pretty soon all of those support networks will return to their normal business, and the Arthurs will be on their own.

Time. It once was mine to do with what I pleased. Or maybe I just lived under the illusion that it was, blithely going through each day thinking, *First I'll do this, then I'll do that, then I'll do the other thing,* as if I had some kind of meteorological control over the forces of nature. Interruptions were annoying and sometimes incredibly stressful, but they, too, would pass. I could return to my normal routine. Not so with the force of nature that has just taken over our lives. This is more than an interruption: this is a radical remaking of who we are. If it wasn't obvious enough in my bodily changes, it shows up in the clock.

But the truth is, none of these things were mine to begin with. Time has never been my own. Each day, each hour, each minute belongs to God. And he's remarkably casual about it. As the Bible suggests in Psalm 90:4, what are to us whole millennia are merely a passing moment to God. Perhaps that's why he's able to offer us the gift of time so freely, so generously. When God is the source of anything, it is enough. It is more than enough. He has, you might say, all the time in the world.

The midnight feedings, the inconvenient diaper blowouts: all of these are trumpet blasts signaling that I'm not the center of the universe. It would be easy to assume that means the baby is in charge, but I'm beginning to suspect God has another lesson, one of his quiet presence in the midst of interruptions, challenging me to accept what I didn't recognize was a gift in the first place: *time*.

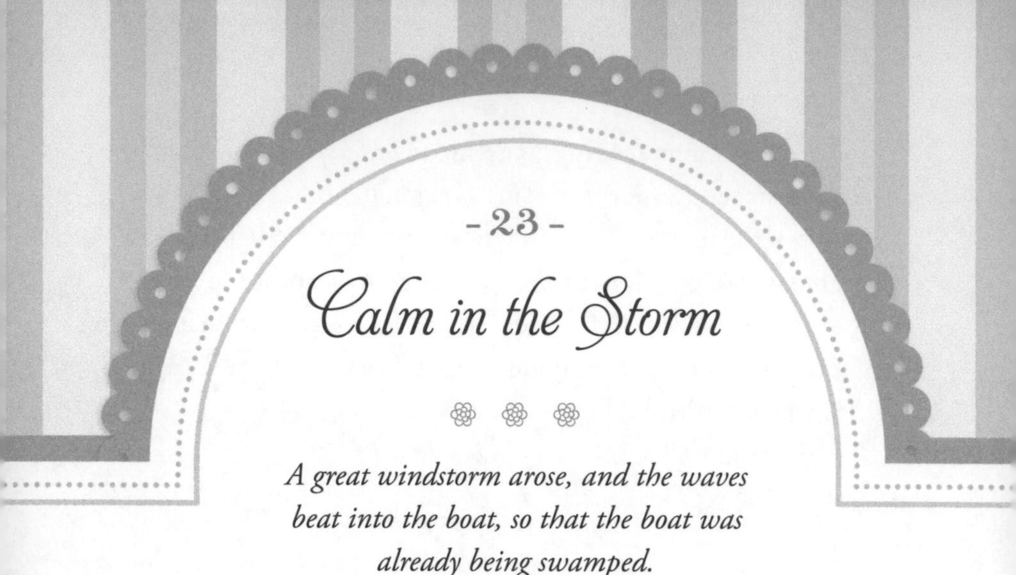

-23-

Calm in the Storm

❀ ❀ ❀

A great windstorm arose, and the waves beat into the boat, so that the boat was already being swamped.

MARK 4:37 (NRSV)

I LOVE THAT PHRASE from today's Scripture, "already being swamped." It doesn't show up in every translation, but when it does, it stands out. Because it's describing my life. I wake up in the morning—or at whatever time my day officially "starts," thanks to my newborn—and before I've even gotten out of bed, my life is *already* being swamped. I can almost imagine water sloshing over the sides of the bed, the mattress rocking violently on a stormy sea. Baby, laundry, meals, dishes, a bathroom shower sporting some creepy pink growth—all of the million things I need to do threatening to drown me. And I haven't even put my feet on the floor yet. When did life become a Category 5 hurricane?

It reminds me of a marvelous quote by C. S. Lewis, which I've kept on a card for most of my adult life. He talks about how when we first wake up in the morning, all our cares and hopes come rushing at us "like wild animals":

> The first job each morning consists simply in shoving them all back; in listening to that other voice, taking that other point of view, letting that other larger, stronger, quieter life come flowing in. And so on, all day. Standing back from all your natural fussings and frettings; coming in out of the wind.[1]

Coming in out of the wind. That's exactly what I crave. When my boat is already being swamped, I want to beat back the waves, row to calmer waters, stand back from all my "natural fussings and frettings." I want that other, calmer, steadier life to come washing in, like a fresh tide.

The problem is, my "fussings" are exactly what Lewis says: *natural.* They are part of my personality. They are not the result of my chaotic life; they are born of the human tendency to fret and my own tendency to stew and obsess. They are a reminder that I must discipline my mind and heart to focus on what's really important, to cultivate and practice gratitude, to take a deep breath and bear witness to God's work in the midst of the mess.

When the disciples saw Jesus asleep in the stern in Mark 4:38, waves crashing around them, they were justifiably freaked out. How could he sleep through all this? They woke him, ready to dump their fussings and frettings onto somebody who should be freaking out too. "Teacher," they shrieked, "don't you care that we're going to drown?" Notice how they didn't ask—or even expect—him to help, merely to share in the general panic. And notice, too, how he didn't answer their question, which was a stupid one anyway, but instead addressed the immediate problem by calming the storm (see verse 39). There. Done. And you were saying . . . ?

So, on those days when life with a baby threatens to swamp my boat, it's not enough to simply tell Jesus how stressed out I am. I need to ask him to help.

- 24 -

Quiet Time

Before daybreak the next morning, Jesus got up and went out to an isolated place to pray.

MARK 1:35

I'M NOT SURE WHERE this came from, but somewhere in my past I learned that having a "personal quiet time with God" was vitally important for the Christian life. Chalk it up to having a pastor for a father or attending an evangelical college—whatever the case, the ideal of daily quiet time was more than a mere suggestion: it was an expectation. This is what Christians do. If we are serious about our faith—if we really love Jesus—then we take time for him every day.

The Bible does not use the phrase *quiet time*, although there are references all throughout Scripture to finding solitary places for prayer and Bible study (see today's verse). But the minute I hear the phrase, a particular ideal springs to mind, the perfect "quiet time." Tell me if this sounds familiar:

I awake on a leisurely, sunny morning (it's always sunny in my ideal) and make my way to the kitchen, where coffee or tea has magically been prepared. I pour myself a cup, then stroll into my sunroom (I don't have a sunroom, but doesn't that sound nice?) and sit on something tastefully comfortable, a wicker rocker, perhaps, with French chic fabric. There I open my Bible and drink deeply of God's Word, pausing after many long moments to check my watch. "Look at the time!" I exclaim. "I should probably start writing in my journal!" It's a prayer journal, of course (not that I've kept one in years), so I start scribbling all my praises and prayer requests, able to focus intently on talking with God. I close with reading a devotional book or two, then tidy up my "quiet time" corner with a sigh, ready to face the day.

Sounds lovely, doesn't it?

Lovely, and totally unrealistic, even *without* a newborn. Most days I am awakened against my will. I feed and change the baby, stumble out into the kitchen, and wonder how it is that dirty dishes have appeared *already* (was someone eating in the middle of the *night*?). I snatch something to chew on—forget traditional breakfast food: leftover pizza will do—and then eat with one hand, holding the baby in the other. If I manage to get anything else done besides child care (such as, say, transferring clothes from the washer to the dryer), I consider the day a success.

Quiet time? Not so much. Solitude? Never. I know this is a season, that eventually my son will settle into a nap routine and I'll find my rhythm again, but in the meantime I can't shake the loads of spiritual guilt I heap onto myself whenever I fail the ideal.

And maybe that's the problem. Maybe the ideal is not

something God wants in the first place. Maybe what he wants right now is not long stretches of my undivided attention (get in line, please) but a simple attentiveness to his presence in the midst of the chaos.

Not quite a sunroom with chic wicker, but a worthy goal nonetheless.

-25-

While You Were Eating

Let all that I am wait quietly before God,
for my hope is in him.

PSALM 62:5

IF EVER THERE WAS a long stretch of nothingness in the care of infants, it would be during the feeding process. I know kids get more efficient at this eventually, but in the meantime it's at least a forty-five-minute ordeal in which I maybe have the use of one hand, if I'm lucky. Since it's impossible to hold a book open and turn its pages one-handed (yes, an e-reader and smartphone are on my Christmas list), I have settled for watching all the DVDs we own, which are pathetically few. But I don't always manage to get the movie queued up before my son completely falls apart, at which point I plop down in the nearest convenient spot, hoping that a glass of water, if nothing else, is within reach.

And then comes the long waiting, the test of my ability to do nothing. If my brain were more alert, I could recite poetry, perhaps, or map out the draft of my next book. I could spend the hour in deep, soul-searching prayer. But sleep deprivation has ensured that my mental energy is at an all-time low. I couldn't recite my full name if you asked me. I end up settling for a small, silent battle over which emotion will take control: resentment or gratitude. If I manage the latter, I consider that a victory.

Waiting: the nemesis of our frenetic culture and not exactly my favorite pastime. And yet not only is it a regular feature of life with a newborn, it has the distinction of being something the Bible honors as an important spiritual discipline.

Granted, when the Scriptures speak of waiting, they usually refer to waiting on the Lord, waiting for God to act. Passages like Isaiah 8:17, Lamentations 3:26, and James 5:7 remind us that waiting is a good thing, an act of hope—even, in some cases, an act of defiance against the distracting and destroying powers of this world.

But Psalm 62:5, today's Scripture, takes the act of waiting even further. It's not merely a symbolic gesture, a simple matter of self-restraint as one goes about one's regular business. Rather, it's a whole-body experience. "Let *all that I am* wait quietly before God," the psalmist says (emphasis added). Not just my brain shifting into a different mode. Not just going about my business while inwardly craving God's intervention. But *all of me*, body and brain, plopping down in the nearest spot for a long stretch of nothingness.

It might be odd to equate this kind of waiting with what mothers of newborns experience, but I've begun to suspect that bodily trials can be a school for the soul. Which means I should be some kind of spiritual genius when this is all over. . . .

-26-

Cultivating Mindfulness

You made all the delicate, inner parts of my body
and knit me together in my mother's womb.

PSALM 139:13

I TALKED WITH MY HUSBAND recently about how I want to cultivate mindfulness of God's presence in the midst of daily activities. After all, Tom is in this mess, too, carrying some of the load through bottle-feeding and midnight diaper changes and general housework. When I mentioned my struggle to him, he said, "Oh, I've been trying to do that." And then he went on to describe how he prays for Micah while giving him a bottle.

By his description, Tom rests his hands on our son and prays for the different parts of Micah's body as symbols of what Tom hopes Micah will become. He prays for Micah's legs, that he will stand strong in the Lord; for Micah's knees, that he will be the sort of person who kneels in prayer; for his tummy, that he will feed on God's Word; and so on, from bottom to top. Since the exercise involves sight, touch, and an obvious progression of ideas, Tom is able to stay relatively focused. It's a manageable discipline.

I listened to his description with a mixture of astonishment and jealousy. In all the hours I have spent feeding the baby, it never once occurred to me to pray like that. Sure, my body and hormones are in a different zone most of the time, turning me into Momzilla. There are numerous brain cells that have vanished, never to be retrieved again. But part of me wants to keep my spirituality intact enough to come up with something this creative, this meaningful.

Because Micah's body really is amazing. Is there anything so astonishing as a newborn ear? It was one of the first things to sprout onto his miniature head while in the womb, and it was fully functioning before birth, allowing him to become familiar with the voices of both his parents—if a bit muffled—before we met him. Now it rests, slightly crumpled, against his fringe of hair, one of the key ways that Micah encounters his world. I've studied it in amazement: now it's time to turn that amazement into an exclamation of thanksgiving. God made this. Praise Him!

Psalm 139 captures this response in one of the most beautiful passages in all of Scripture. I've mentioned this psalm already several times, but it's today's verse, 13, that captures the sense of mindfulness in the midst of everyday life. You can almost picture the psalmist observing his own hands in awe, then gazing at the body of his newborn son. All *this*—this ordinary, taken-for-granted life—it's all God's handiwork.

I want to be aware of these little details, mindful of the

holy in the midst of the ordinary. It's a battle that I lose more often than I win right now. But I'm hopeful it won't always be like this. In the end, I'm grateful that one of us is able to pray, at least!

- 27 -

Hear Our Prayer

O Lord, please hear my prayer!
Listen to the prayers of those of us
who delight in honoring you.

NEHEMIAH 1:11

WHILE LIVING IN AN INTENTIONAL Christian community during graduate school, my husband and I picked up the habit of evening prayer. Every night after the babies and toddlers were asleep, the couples and singles who shared our household would gather in the living room and light some candles. We'd sing a few songs, read a few Scriptures, and then lift up our praises and requests, closing with the Lord's Prayer while holding hands in a circle. There was nothing dramatic about it—often there were more yawns of exhaustion than coherent sentences—but the rhythm of sharing that simple routine became deeply embedded in our lives.

Tom and I have carried that rhythm into other settings ever since: to our hometown in northern Michigan, where we stayed one summer while Tom served as interim pastor;

to our vacations in various places; and now to our current home in southern Michigan.

When we first moved here a few years ago, we continued using *The Book of Common Prayer*, a little handbook for congregational and household worship used for centuries by many Christians around the world. We had modified it, by this time, but the basic structure was there: recite a psalm, read some Scripture, pray, close with the Lord's Prayer. No matter what else was going on—even if we had company over—we would pause before bedtime and pray, company included, if they wished.

Right before Micah was born we were reading through sections from the book of Nehemiah each night. It's not a long book: thirteen chapters, to be precise. My parents, who had come to visit for my birthday and other events, joined us for prayer, my pastor-father chuckling when we reached Nehemiah 11 and it was his turn to read (nothing like endless lists of Hebrew names to test all that seminary training!). Then Micah made a surprise entrance, and everything fell apart.

We have made some valiant attempts to revive evening prayer. At first I nodded off during Nehemiah 12 (more names!); and then we went several weeks without hearing what happened to the returned exiles. More than a month later my parents have come to stay with us again, and we are *still* in Nehemiah. Maybe it's time to throw in the towel.

Well, not entirely—just the towel of that particular pattern. Yes, we'll still try to pray at night, but maybe just the Lord's Prayer, with Micah in his footed sleeper. And maybe we'll only nail it once every four days or so, on average. But that's better than never. And much better than going another two months wondering what happened to Nehemiah, all the while feeling like spiritual losers.

Evening prayer may not be a detailed, involved thing anymore—or at least, not for a long time. But, like Nehemiah, we can ask that God will hear our prayers anyway.

-28-
Three-Breath Prayer

May the grace of the Lord Jesus Christ, the love of God, and the fellowship of the Holy Spirit be with you all.

2 CORINTHIANS 13:14

I RECENTLY WATCHED an online video of a mom teaching her young kids a Bible story. They sat on the floor together, the storytelling props in front of them, and the mom said something like, "Before we hear this story, let's take a moment to focus our hearts on God." Then she taught them what she called a three-breath prayer.

"We're going to take a deep breath, like we're trying to inhale all the air in this room, and then we're going to blow it out like we're trying to push a big ship across the ocean. Ready?"

They all took a breath, and she said, "In the name of the Father," and they blew it out; then again, "In the name of the Son"—whoosh; and again, "In the name of the Holy Spirit, Amen." By the time they were done, their little bodies were relaxed, their faces calm and attentive. And I was in awe.

Three simple breaths, three simple phrases. In less than a minute, a Trinitarian affirmation not only of what God gives us (breath, life) but of who God is (Father, Son, and Holy Spirit). After all my agonizing new-mother guilt over my inability to find a decent stretch of time to spend with God every day (see pp. 63–73), this three-breath prayer is like a free gift card, a voucher good for endless moments in the presence of God.

The apostle Paul, while writing words of challenge and encouragement to the Christians in the ancient city of Corinth, penned this blessing, which is one of my favorites: "May the grace of the Lord Jesus Christ, the love of God, and the fellowship of the Holy Spirit be with you all" (2 Corinthians 13:14). I can almost imagine Paul breathing in and out with each phrase: inhaling grace, exhaling guilt; inhaling love, exhaling bitterness; inhaling fellowship, exhaling alienation.

Not that I'm an expert in hot yoga or anything. But breathing seems doable. I don't have to have my peaceful sunroom and cup of coffee. I don't have to carve an hour out of my already shattered schedule. I don't even have to put down the baby. I can just breathe. Breathe in the presence of God, breathe out my frustration. Breathe in gratitude for the simple graces, breathe out my fears. It can be a prayer of petition; it can be a prayer of blessing. I can say it while feeding my insatiable child; I can say it while changing a diaper. I can say it for the rest of my life, when Micah is asking for the car keys or walking down the wedding aisle.

Breathe. Now *that* I can do.

– 29 –

Thirst

As the deer longs for streams of water,
so I long for you, O God.

PSALM 42:1

THIRST. They warned me about this, all those nursing moms. They told me that breastfeeding is thirsty business, and they weren't kidding. I wake up thirsty, I go to bed thirsty, I holler for water when I've landed in a random location to nurse my child and there's not a cup or mug or bottle to be seen. My skin is dry; I feel like I'm wrinkling up like a raisin. One of these days I'll wake up and I will have turned into a camel.

Thirst was a problem back when I was pregnant, too. But that was trickier. If I didn't drink enough, I got those crazy practice contractions that sent me pacing the floor, wondering if I was going to deliver the baby too soon. But if I drank too much, I had to pee every fifteen minutes, which was not exactly helpful while, say, on a road trip to a wedding in Chicago when I was eight months pregnant—or, say, while I was *in* the wedding itself. I had to learn to take lots of little sips: just enough to keep me going but not enough to send me dashing to the restroom.

Now I can't guzzle enough. I am constantly spying out water sources. I know where all the drinking fountains are in every grocery store, clinic, mall, or library in a thirty-mile radius. I'm like a little creature that has beaten a path to every watering hole around, like the deer in today's Scripture passage. Water has become a matter of survival—well, it always has been, but now my body gives me stronger signals, in part because if I don't listen my baby suffers too. I need it. I can't live without it. I will move heaven and earth to get it.

Today's verse from Psalm 42 convicts me. Because I don't know that I've ever longed for God as much as I've longed for water lately. I know I need him. I know that I can't survive without him. I even know that my baby can't live without God. And there have been moments in my life—dark moments—when the only thing that got me through was the knowledge that God was there, that God in Christ has suffered too. But I must acknowledge that deep down, I do not crave God's presence like I should.

Why is that? Where does the longing for God come from? Perhaps it comes from deprivation, when so many comforts are taken away that we turn to God because we find sustenance nowhere else. Perhaps it comes from desperation, when we are so beaten down that we have no one else to turn to. Perhaps it comes from a slow lifetime of realizing that of all our many blessings, only God truly satisfies.

What will it take for me to seek God the way a nursing mom seeks water?

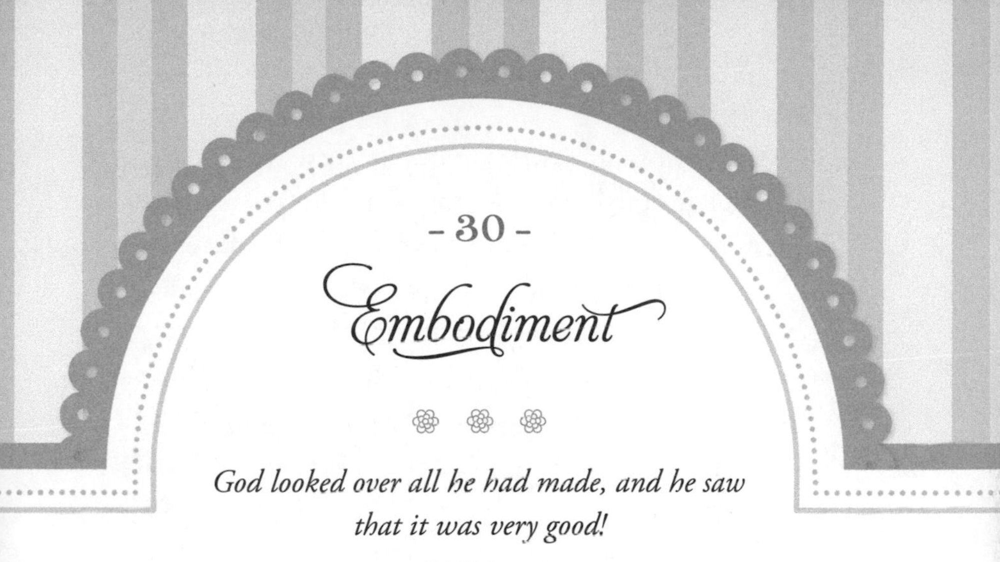

- 30 -
Embodiment

God looked over all he had made, and he saw that it was very good!

GENESIS 1:31

NO ONE PREPARES you for the sheer physicality of pregnancy and motherhood. Unless you live in a litter of puppies, you are never touched so often, so relentlessly, in so many places that are otherwise off limits, by everyone from total strangers (hello, male ob-gyn intern who can't be more than twenty-four) to your immediate family.

And it's not just the touching. There's the physical endurance required in dragging yourself out of bed at two in the morning for an unknown number of minutes or hours—and then functioning the rest of the waking day. There's the muscle strength required in lifting seven or ten or fifteen pounds—up, down, across, over, all day long—plus the weight of various equipment that never unfolds or clicks or rolls or rocks the way you need it to. And I have yet to finish a meal. If someone asks how I'm doing, I say, "I'm starving," which is an unvaried response from when I was pregnant.

All of this serves to remind me that I am, in fact, more than just a brain. I am more than just the sum of my intellectual achievements, the thoughts running around in my head. I am a body; I am embodied. I have what the biblical authors call flesh. Bones and muscles, ligaments and veins, bodily organs and an outer shell of skin. I am a physical being inhabiting this physical world, with all the needs and cravings and instincts of the animal kingdom.

Most of the time, we humans have a pretty poor understanding of what embodiment means. On the one hand we place far too much emphasis on the body, glorying in its beauty or desires, elevating the sensual above all things. We women in particular have become the receptacles of far too many millennia of human body worship, inheriting a distorted view of what our bodies are for and what they are supposed to look like. Especially postpregnancy: if I see another online article about how to lose the baby fat, I just might throw something. What if baby fat is a mark of honor? A sign of participating with God in something remarkable? A battle scar?

Humans can also fall into the other error about the body, which is to treat it as something inherently bad, not worth caring about. The soul, some say, is of far more worth, has far more eternal value, than these transitory, decaying, corrupt physical bodies. The flesh is sinful. Deny and tame the body: focus instead on cultivating the mind, nurturing the soul. Really? I guess that leaves out most moms, then, who can't avoid embodiment as a daily practice.

Into all this mess steps God the Creator. Far from seeing embodiment as a liability, God looks at the material world he has made—including human beings—and calls our bodies "very good" (see today's Scripture). Not divine enough to worship, not evil enough to denigrate, but *very good.*

So, how am I doing these days? I'm hungry, thank God. Pass the peanut butter.

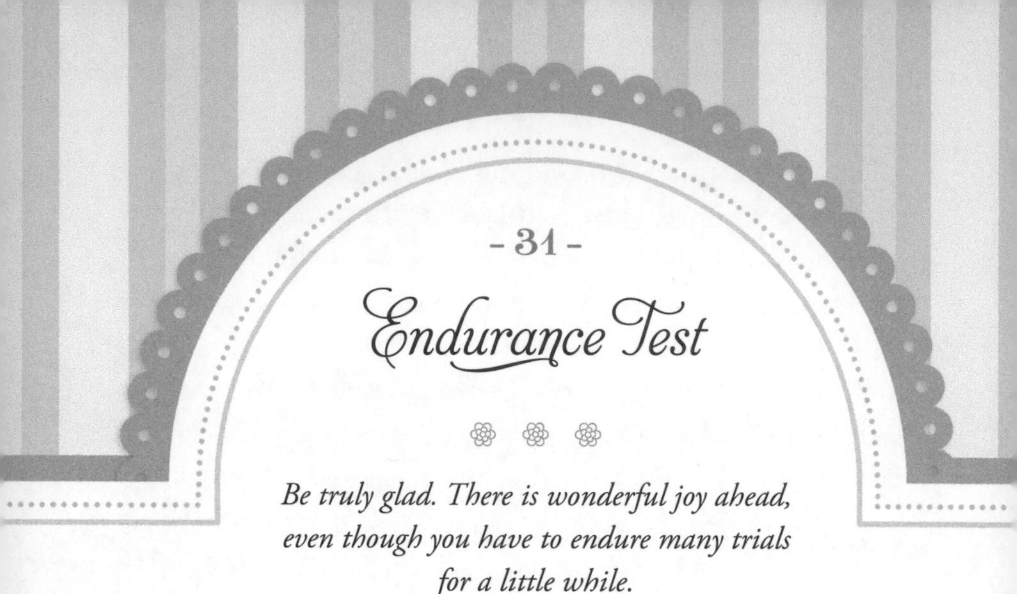

- 31 -

Endurance Test

Be truly glad. There is wonderful joy ahead, even though you have to endure many trials for a little while.

I PETER 1:6

I'VE DECIDED THAT BECOMING a parent is like learning a new sport. First you have to acquire all the gear and learn how to use it. Then comes the test of your physical endurance, the moving of muscles you didn't know you had, the soreness, the exhaustion, the general discouragement when you watch those people who are pros. And of course, just when you feel like you've maybe got the hang of it, the intensity ramps up a level, and another level, and another. All for a sport you aren't even sure you enjoy half the time.

It reminds me of when my husband and I decided to start backpacking. We read all the pertinent information, told our family and friends about it, acquired the piles of gear. We selected the trails, mapped out the journey, began packing and even weight training, hoping to be in the best possible shape. In anticipation we took short little trips close to home, just to practice, and even walked around the house with our packs and boots on, getting used to the weight and breaking our boots in slowly.

But then came the real thing. Then came the actual moment when we gazed up at the mountain pass, set our feet on the trail, and began to hike. I'm not an athlete by nature, so it was enough just to concentrate on my next breath, much less my next step. And my pack was soooooo heavy. I was ready for our first break after a mile. When we set up the tent later that evening, I crawled into my sleeping bag and didn't want to move again.

Of course, the scenery made up for nearly everything, especially in retrospect. Looking back on those first few backpacking trips—flipping through the photo albums—I am in awe of the beauty and grandeur we were privileged to witness. All the miles seemed worth it when we arrived at an overlook or came upon a surprise patch of wildflowers growing from bare rock. Granted, I could have done without the storms and rain (wet socks and I do not get along), but those difficult moments were few and have since smoothed out in my memory. My life was enriched; I am a better person for those adventures. I would do it all over again.

And maybe that's what parenting an infant is like. Maybe all the hard stuff, like learning new gear and putting your body to the test, smooths out in retrospect, seems like nothing in the face of the beautiful and amazing moments. Someday I'll look back on these days or flip through our photos and see only the gorgeousness of my child, the tenderness of our intimate time together.

What seems like a serious trial of embodiment now may become, over time, the very stuff that shapes my character, enriches my life, makes me a better person. "There is wonderful joy ahead," the apostle Peter promises in today's Scripture passage. For that, I would do it all over again.

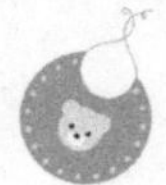

– 32 –

Matter MATTERS

The Word became human and made his home among us.

JOHN 1:14

I'VE SPENT A LOT of my life living inside my head. I'm a reader, for one: as a kid I spent hours and hours with my nose in books, pausing only to go to the bathroom when I was really desperate. Then as I grew older, I indulged in my writing hobby, which grew into a habit, which grew into a vocation. Writers spend a lot of time inside their own heads, following trains of thought all over the landscape of the interior life, surfacing occasionally to grab a snack.

And then I went to graduate school, which was the ultimate brainy indulgence. I would emerge from the university library blinking in the southern sunshine like a bat, as if I'd been holed up in a cave all day. Which was kind of true. It would take the first five minutes of my walk back to the parking lot to clear the cobwebs and remind me that I was, in fact, treading the real earth on a real day in the current century, with real flowers blooming along the real stone wall and real people passing by.

Within a year after grad school I got pregnant, and suddenly my body trumped my brain. My days were no longer driven by the pursuit of ideas but were taken up with bodily functions, such as where to find the nearest bathroom. I spent far too many hours a day just feeding myself. Sleep became my dearest desire. I was more aware than ever that I am embodied, that we human beings are in fact human *beings*, not just walking brains.

Things haven't changed since having a baby. Embodiment is my daily MO. I am becoming more and more comfortable with my own flesh. And not "flesh" as the biblical euphemism for the sinful side of human nature, but as a physical reality that God has made holy by taking on flesh himself.

Theologians call it the *Incarnation*, the moment when God took on a body and dwelt among us in the person of Jesus Christ. The word comes from the Latin *carne*, which means "meat" or "flesh." The apostle John speaks of this in the opening chapter of his Gospel, reminding us that God not only took on flesh but lived among us (see today's Scripture).

Writes Debra Rienstra in her marvelous book *Great with Child: On Becoming a Mother*, "One of the most profound and far-reaching implications of the Christian belief that God both created the world and entered it personally, is that matter *matters*; it has inherent meaning."[1] The ground I tread, the hands I reach with to hold my baby's body, the food I eat . . . all of it is matter that *matters*. Because God has touched it. God bothered to walk the ground, hold a hand, bless a child, eat a meal.

So rather than become exasperated by all this embodiment, I can see it as yet another opportunity to grow closer to the God who made us.

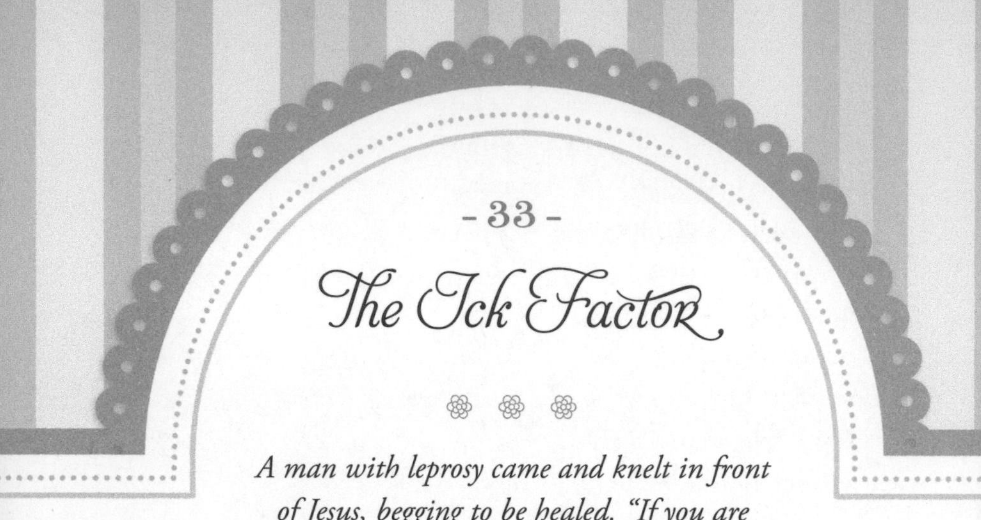

- 33 -
The Ick Factor

A man with leprosy came and knelt in front of Jesus, begging to be healed. "If you are willing, you can heal me and make me clean," he said. Moved with compassion, Jesus reached out and touched him. "I am willing," he said. "Be healed!"

MARK 1:40-41

JUST WHEN I'M BECOMING reconciled to the idea of embodiment, to life in a material zone in which matter *matters* (see previous devo), my son spits up. Again. For the fifteenth time this morning. Sure, I understand that God has created our bodies and called them good. I get that embodiment can be a spiritual discipline. But spit-up? Seriously?

I won't even go into all the other bodily secretions—both his and mine—that I'm now more familiar with than I ever wanted to be. Becoming a mother has turned me into part chemist, part sanitation worker: bottling and storing, wiping and cleaning, sterilizing and flushing. Of the ten most common words I use in a given day, *Ew* is at the top of the list. This, among many others, is the reason I'm not an RN.

So where does all this embodiment take me? How do I take the ick factor and see it as something God uses to draw me closer to him? Perhaps it starts with Jesus himself—not just his own birth and infancy, which I have to believe were just as icky as every other baby's, but the very choice of God to become human in the first place. God, who could have kept himself above the fray, above the mess and madness, chose to enter our ick, to take on our bodily fluids, and even, as today's Scripture suggests, to touch the untouchable ick of others.

A man born blind is given sight when Jesus makes a paste of his own spit and dirt and rubs it on the man's eyes. A woman who has been hemorrhaging for twelve years touches the fringe of his garment, hoping for a secret blessing, and he heals her. A leper, an epileptic, a corpse—all of these bodies that the society of Jesus' day would have considered physically and religiously "unclean"—he touches without compunction, without (it seems) even the slightest shiver. As the disciples turn away and mutter, "Ew," Jesus finds the body worthy enough to touch. Even the ick.

He could have healed the leper—oozing with open sores and wounds—without touching him. But he didn't. He reached out. He was, in his own words, "willing." It would be easy to dismiss this as some sort of personality quirk, as if he'd make a great EMT had he lived in a different millennium. But I'm beginning to realize that if Jesus was fully human, as our creeds and Scriptures claim, then his willingness to embrace the body was probably just as much a spiritual discipline for him as it is for me. Which means I need his help. Daily. Hourly. Spit-up by spit-up.

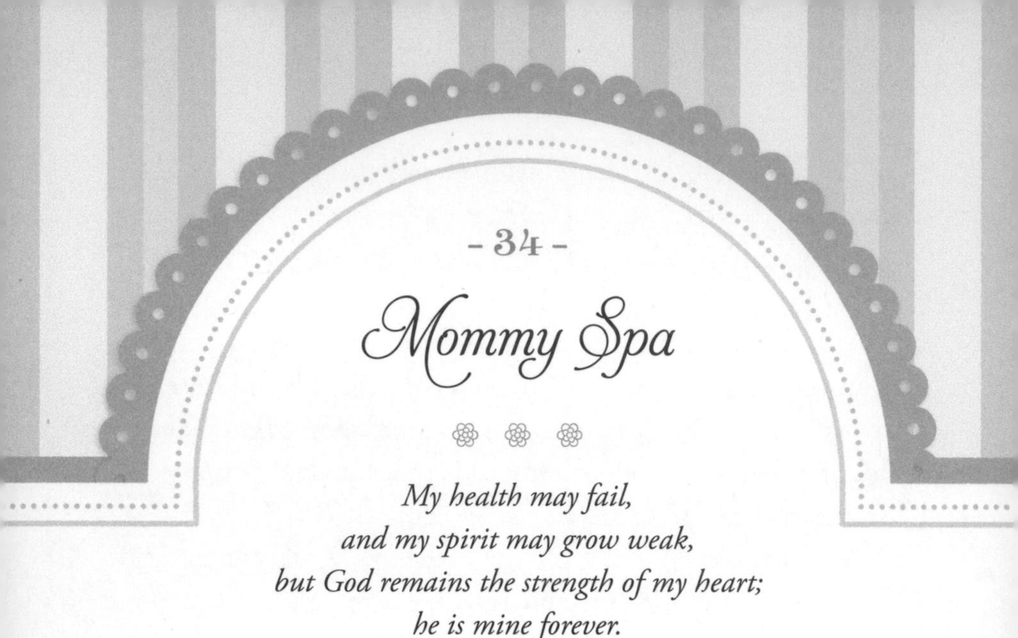

- 34 -

Mommy Spa

My health may fail,
and my spirit may grow weak,
but God remains the strength of my heart;
he is mine forever.

PSALM 73:26

WHEN MY HUSBAND CAME home from work today, I handed him the monitor and said in queenly tones, "*I* am taking a bath." It has been months since I've taken anything but a quick shower, thanks to the fact that the only tub in our house is in the guest bathroom, which has been in constant use since Micah was born. But today I'd had enough. Between the freezing winter weather, Micah's relentless spit-up, and numerous online posts about spa treatments my friends have had lately, I decided it was time *this* mommy indulged herself, for once.

So I ran the bathwater, poured in some aroma-therapy salts, lit a few candles, and settled in for a nice long soak. It was lovely. It was luxurious. It was indulgent. It was slightly guilt inducing, but that's because (as radio personality Garrison

Keillor would say) I'm from the Midwest and have Lutheran roots. Plus, I'm a mother, and mothers like to feel guilty about something. But I was determined to enjoy myself.

Many blissful minutes later I stepped out of the tub, dried off, snuffed out the candles, and emerged triumphantly from the bathroom. The baby was still asleep; all was right with the world. I had done it! I had indulged myself! Hurray for Mommy Time!

That's when the fire alarm went off.

Yep, the snuffed-out candles set off the alarm just outside the bathroom door, triggering all the other alarms in the house. If I had successfully beaten back any guilt before, it all descended again in force. It took my husband and me several minutes to stop the alarms from clanging, during which the baby, bless him, slept like a champ. But before it was over, I had vowed never to take a bath again. So much for Mommy Time.

Of course, I don't seriously believe the fire alarm was some kind of punishment for indulging myself. I believe that caring for my body is part of caring for my son, who depends on me for nourishment, comfort, and strength. If I don't eat well, Micah suffers physically. If I don't sleep well, Micah suffers emotionally from a weary, snappish mother. If I don't nurture my spiritual life, Micah suffers in his spirit.

At the same time, caring for my body is not the same as indulging it. Yes, I can and should take a relaxing bath now and then. But it is not some kind of cherished right that is being violated by the demands of motherhood. The fact that

I don't have a weekly pedicure is not some sort of deprivation: it's just life—well, and a lifestyle choice. Bodies are bodies: they aren't gods. Someday my body will fail me utterly, and then I will know, as Psalm 73:26 says, that it is *God* who has been the strength of my heart, not whatever I've managed in the way of pampering.

- 35 -

Big Bad World

I prayed to the LORD, *and he answered me.*
He freed me from all my fears.

PSALM 34:4

SOMETIMES I MISS the whole pregnant thing. There was something about all those strangers opening doors for me that made me believe the world isn't completely going down the drain. *If men can do this,* I thought in my endorphin-induced euphoria, *they can conquer terrorism.*

Now when I carry my infant son around, my mother-bear instincts kick in. Every stranger is a homicidal maniac or a Typhoid Mary. Why, oh why, must every person in the grocery store decide that the best way to welcome my small child into the world is to touch his face or fingers? *Thank you* for exposing him to vast colonies of disease, to the lingering juices from raw meat, to a universe of unsavory sanitation practices. Fantastic.

This goes back to my postpartum terror about the world in general, the feeling that no place is safe except the three-foot by three-foot section of our bedroom that houses the bassinet. I am all animal, ready to snarl. Doorbell ringing? It's the mail guy, whose job is to transport gastroenteritis from house to house. (There's nothing more sinister than those two simple words, "Sign here." Must I? Must I handle that writing utensil? Really?) Car approaching the intersection in front of us? Driver is wasted, no doubt, three sheets to the wind and it's only two in the afternoon. Who *are* these people?

Well, they're the same ones who opened doors and carried my grocery bags and waved me across the street when I was pregnant. They're the same ones who gave up their seats on the bus and even, unaccountably, handed me a potted plant for free. Just because. The world hasn't changed: it still has its good folks and bad folks, health and disease. No, I'm the one who has changed. I'm the one with the crazy hormones and the sudden phobia of touching ATMs and the weird dreams that I've left Micah with total strangers (see "Free Agent," pp. 43–44).

Thankfully God is still God, still in charge, and in fact designed me with all the motherly instincts that have turned me into a complete freak. He is not surprised by any of this. He does not think I am somehow less spiritual, less human, less of a woman of faith because my body has suddenly trumped my brain. He calls me to give my anxieties to him, to turn my worries into prayers so that, as the psalmist says, I can have freedom from fear (see Psalm 34:4).

So in the midst of my own craziness, I sense a deep well of patience and grace, a gentle reminder that this is merely a season, that even the hormones are a gift. Yes, I need to be cautious, but God really has put some of these people here to help.

Will I still wipe down the shopping cart—the *whole thing*, not just the handle—with those complimentary wipes? You bet.

- 36 -
It Happened to Me

Give all your worries and cares to God,
for he cares about you.
1 PETER 5:7

SOMEONE GAVE ME a subscription to a popular parenting magazine, which is basically just one big flyer full of advertisements with maybe five paragraphs of helpful parenting tips. One of its columns is about true things that happened to real parents, called "It Happened to Me." Parents submit stories about how a long strand of hair got wound around their daughter's finger and she had to be rushed to the ER, or how a pot of boiling water fell on a baby at a restaurant.

I suppose, in some weird way, those stories are meant to be helpful, reminding us to be vigilant and smart. But all they do is keep me up at night, rigid with terror, wondering if our furnace is leaking poisonous gases all over the basement, or if that little bit of glitter from a Christmas card has somehow lodged itself in my son's eye. All I can think is that I could end up in that column, telling my story of how the very worst thing I could imagine did, in fact, happen to me.

So my husband has come up with a remedy. First, I need to stop reading that stupid column. As soon as I see the heading, I flip the page. Second, he has decided someone should write "It Happened to Me: Caveman Edition." You know, vignettes about how our baby was carried off by a herd of wild boar (we rescued him), or how those berries that we thought were tasty were actually hallucinogenic. After I get over the initial horror of imagining my child in the jaws of a saber-toothed tiger that has mistaken him for one of its cubs, I find the whole thing hilarious, which is the point.

Because the truth is, we could spend our whole parental lives paralyzed with anxiety for our children's safety. Or we could surrender our fears to the dual remedies of laughter and prayer. When the apostle Paul says in 1 Peter 5:7 to "give all your worries and cares to God," he's not being sentimental: he really means it. Some translations say, "cast your cares upon him": in other words, throw those suckers at the Lord. As hard and fast as you can. God can handle it.

I cannot protect my son from all the mishaps that could possibly happen to him. And, quite frankly, compared to the vast majority of parents in the world, the list of possible mishaps is tame and manageable (*somewhere* there is a mom who worries about wild boar). Yes, I do need to be smart and vigilant. I check his tiny digits for strands of hair; and, when he is bigger, I will make sure he is not within grabbing distance of hot beverages. All of those reflexes will have become instinctual.

But so, I hope, will have become the impulse to pray. Daily. Hourly. By the minute. For God to intercede, to watch, to give me wisdom. And laughter.

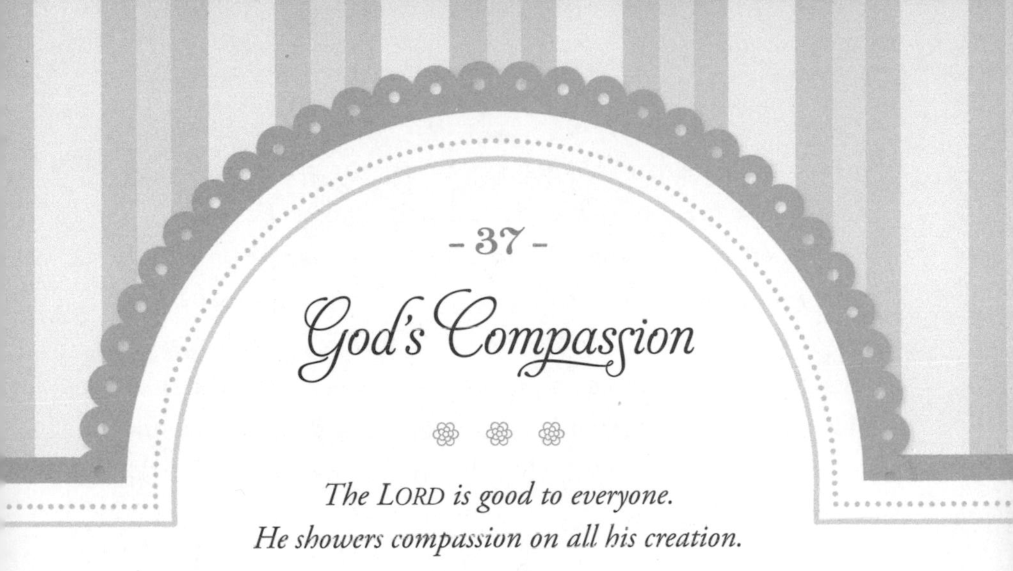

- 37 -

God's Compassion

The LORD is good to everyone.
He showers compassion on all his creation.

PSALM 145:9

I DON'T KNOW if it's a mom thing, or the hormones, or the recent trauma to my body, but it's as if I can feel every grief and terror in the world. Headlines about natural disasters send my heart racing. All I can think of is the children. News about a child who is sick—a child I don't even know, someone on the news, a cancer victim—makes me pause at the window, trembling. Why haven't I ever realized before how irreplaceable each human life *is*?

My baby exhales, and I wait for the quiet in-drawing of another breath, and another. The simple act of breathing, which I've taken for granted all my life, is suddenly tenuous. It can stop at any moment. Not merely my own breath—I've had several decades getting used to the idea of my own mortality—but the breath of all things, of this small person, of this little life that I cradled in my body for so many months and whose every movement wrecks my soul.

When do we stop feeling like the anxious mother of the whole world? The suffering of children slays me. I am undone at the mere phrase "pediatric unit." When I hear of parents who have lost a child, I weep and weep and weep. I've always been an empathetic person, but this goes way beyond empathy. This is like carrying the world in your womb and then finding yourself, postdelivery, in the neonatal unit, willing the world to keep breathing. It's like . . . well . . . like suddenly experiencing the world through the heart of God—not just through the *eyes* of God, with a kind of clinical detachment, but through the *heart* of God, the center of who God is, from the well out of which all of God's love and compassion flows.

In Hebrew the word for *compassion* comes from the root word for *womb*.[1] It puts a fascinating spin on passages like Psalm 145, which at first is all about God's mighty kingship—very manly language—and then suddenly switches to the maternal language of verse 9: "He showers compassion on all his creation." It's a comforting image, God's womb-like love for us, surrounding us with all the nourishment and protection that we can't give ourselves. We've done nothing to deserve it: indeed, most of us are unaware of it entirely, just like an unborn child who rests in that care, aware of nothing beyond the warmth and sway and rhythm of life.

Perhaps this is the strange gift of motherhood, or hormones, or whatever this is: that for a brief season I'm given a small glimpse of what God feels for each one of us.

- 38 -

Never Forgotten

Can a mother forget her nursing child?
Can she feel no love for the child she has borne?
But even if that were possible,
I would not forget you!

ISAIAH 49:15

A NUMBER OF YEARS AGO, fresh out of college, I served as the full-time youth director of a fairly large church. There were lots of high points in that experience—not including the time, while on a road trip, that I accidentally left a kid at a gas station.

Yes: you read that correctly.

In my defense, before driving off I asked the vanload of high schoolers if everyone was on board, to which one of the guys in back responded, a bit too casually, "Yep." It wasn't until we were actually getting on the highway that the younger girls broke the conspiracy and shrieked, "Sarah, you forgot Dave!"

I think I bellowed something like, "Why didn't you tell me before we got on the ramp?!?!!" at which point the guys in the backseat erupted in laughter. It took us ten minutes to reach the next exit, circle around, and return to the gas station, where Dave waited, lounging on a pile of tires, feigning nonchalance.

I got the joke and even thought it was funny. It was the parents back home I was worried about. This was before cell phones were common, so there was no danger of the kid making a flurry of panicked calls. But stories still got around. And I never knew how parents were going to react. Some were the kind to say, "I've always wanted to do that!" while others called the pastor about every little mishap.

A lot could happen to a kid in ten minutes while alone at a gas station. Granted, Dave was approaching eighteen, roughly the age of Alexander the Great when he began his military career—so he could have handled almost anything. But the law doesn't care how emotionally or physically mature a minor is: if he or she is under eighteen, all bets are off. And parents are parents, period.

Now, years after that adventure, I study my son's body and find it incomprehensible that anyone could forget about a child or leave him behind. Yes, my brain understands that he will grow up someday into an autonomous young man. I will not be there to track his every move—nor will he want me to (nor will I want to!). Someone, somewhere, could very well leave him at a gas station; and we'll all find it funny. But in the meantime the thought makes me shiver.

I don't know what kind of parent I will be in the future: the kind who laughs at such episodes or reports them (or the kind who pretends to laugh, masking real concern). At the moment, I am what God was referring to when he spoke through the prophet Isaiah about the tenacious memory of mothers, nursing or otherwise (see today's Scripture). I could not forget my infant if I tried.

The good news is, neither can God. He doesn't forget any of us: not my small son, not my worried self, not even Dave resting on the tire pile. Whenever I start to get anxious, I can take a page from Dave's book: sit on the nearest comfortable spot and wait. We are never forgotten.

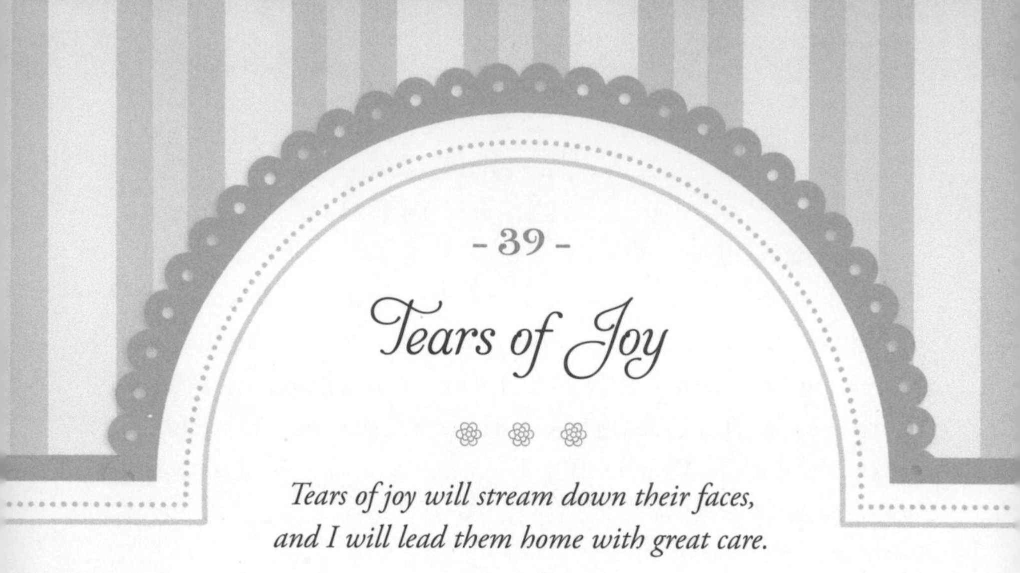

- 39 -

Tears of Joy

Tears of joy will stream down their faces,
and I will lead them home with great care.
JEREMIAH 31:9

THE MORNING I FOUND OUT I was pregnant, my husband was out of town. He had taken a whirlwind trip to Indianapolis to watch Duke beat Butler in the final game of the NCAA basketball tournament and was driving back to Michigan in time for a morning meeting. Already whipped from the drive, the nail-biting agony of a close game, and the sudden euphoria at Duke's win (we're Duke grads), he was totally unprepared for my phone call. Knowing this, I eased into the news, asking about the game and casually double-checking that he was on a relatively safe stretch of road. Then I dropped the bomb.

"I mean, I *think* that's what the pale blue line means," I babbled after his initial pause. "At first I thought the test was defective, but then I looked it up on the Internet, and any blue line in the result window means we're probably pregnant."

"Yeah?" he said, his voice registering mild astonishment. Now, something you need to know about my husband is that he has the outward expressiveness of a Supreme Court judge. For him to register any kind of surprise means that (a) you have just punched him in the kidneys; (b) a large missile is visible in the sky heading for our neighborhood; or (c) Duke has been knocked out of the NCAA basketball championship in the first round by some college no one has ever heard of (ouch).

On the flip side, if there is a cheesy, sappy moment anywhere in a movie, Tom is the one with tears streaming down his face. It doesn't have to be a movie: a life insurance commercial will do. All that emotion, bottled up, converts to liquid and eventually leaks.

After inhaling and exhaling a few times, we went on to discuss the craziness of this information, given that we had only been trying for less than a month. And then we eventually signed off.

He drove to work for his meeting with a colleague, but he was so distracted he finally ended up telling the guy what was going on. "Dude," the guy exclaimed, "go home!" So Tom came home, unexpectedly in the middle of the day, striding through the door with a dozen roses. He knelt and kissed my belly, and we both cried like we were watching the cheesiest life insurance commercial *ever*.

My husband and I have wept together in the past, tears of grief at various losses, tears of anger or fear. On occasion we've wept with happiness or gratitude. Now, as we cried, it was a mixture of joy, surprise, and trepidation. It was saying good-bye to our child-free life (which is not the same as a child*less* life), and adjusting to a new reality. Whatever came of this pregnancy, we were parents. Forever.

Crying seemed in order. And, thanks to today's Scripture, I know God approves. Not only does God approve, but God seems to expect tears when the unannounced good thing happens. No point in bottling it up, trying to go on with a normal day. Revel in the poignancy. Hug your loved ones. Celebrate like it's a national championship. God does!

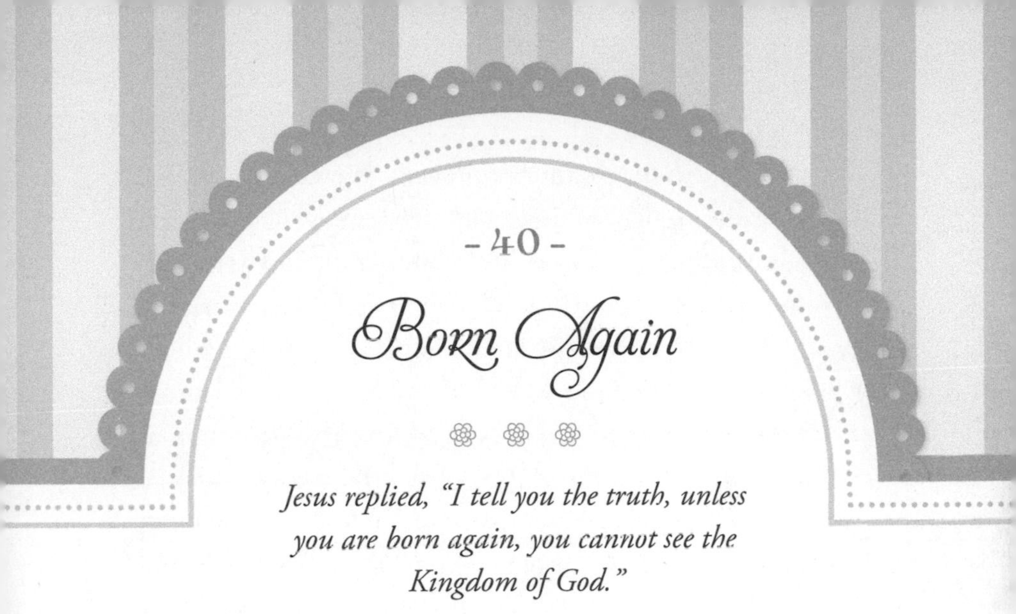

- 40 -

Born Again

Jesus replied, "I tell you the truth, unless you are born again, you cannot see the Kingdom of God."

JOHN 3:3

THERE WAS A DAY, when I was four months pregnant, that I thought I was losing the baby. Nothing medically significant had happened, just some leakage and the frantic feeling I was on the verge of a breakdown. All day I felt like a wartime mother awaiting news of a son or daughter who is MIA.

Ironically, it was Baptism Sunday at our church, when we gather at the lake to welcome new believers and reaffirm our own baptisms. Here I was, silently clinging to my pregnancy with every last ounce of will, and people around me were being born again. The irony was not lost on me.

Today's Scripture is about a man named Nicodemus and his odd midnight visit. John 3 records that the old man, a respected Jewish leader, came under cover of darkness to probe the wisdom of the young rabbi Jesus of Nazareth. Nicodemus came for a lesson but left with a radical overhaul of what it means to live the life of faith. It wasn't just about following the right teaching or merely acknowledging the miraculous presence of God, but about completely starting over. Saying good-bye to the old life—dying to sin, as the apostle Paul says in Romans 6:11—and welcoming a whole new life in Jesus. Being born again.

Usually we think of this process as a kind of free pass to heaven, requiring little work. Yes, we will have new battles to fight against habitual sins. We may mess up from time to time. But we have the required ticket and everything will be okay.

That day at the water's edge, caressing my growing belly, I began to suspect that if birth the first time is hard and harrowing, without guarantees, then new birth into a life of faith must be likewise. Not everyone makes it. The one being born is largely unaware of the depths of love, the depths of self-sacrifice involved. The one being born thinks he or she is doing all the work, when in fact it is the parent who bears the brunt of it.

When Jesus says "you must be born again," there is a hint of the difficult, persevering, heart-wrenching work that God, like a pregnant mother, does on behalf of all who believe. Even Nicodemus misses the hint when he exclaims, "How can an old man go back into his mother's womb and be born again?" (John 3:4)—as if it's the baby's job to conceive himself and make sure he ends up being delivered. And a lot of the time, that's how Christians talk: as if this whole faith thing is up to us, as if being born again is a matter of sheer human willpower as opposed to the strong determination, patience, watchfulness, and grit of our heavenly Parent.

As the folks that day went down into the water and came up again, I felt like bursting into delirious applause. They made it! God pulled it off! I now understood, for the first time, that what we thought was free has cost God everything.

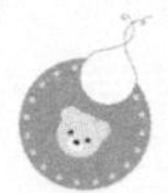

– 41 –

The Long Good-Bye

A sword will pierce your very soul.

LUKE 2:35

IN THE PREVIOUS DEVO, "Born Again," I wrote about how I thought I was losing my pregnancy at four months. It was a harrowing day, fraught with a kind of insane fear that gave every moment a reckless intensity. Eventually I realized that if I didn't want the fear to completely paralyze me, I had to give it up.

There was a moment—I'm not sure what prompted it—when I sailed into calmer water. It was like I had been kayaking on white-water rapids for hours and then suddenly found myself in a smooth, wide oxbow. My jumbled thoughts came together into an overwhelming feeling of gratitude. And it wasn't that I thought my child was okay. It was that I had come to grips with the reality of loss.

I began talking to my unborn baby, telling the child everything a mother wants to say: "Thank you for the privilege of being your mother. I have learned so much from you. I would never trade this experience for a pain-free life. If I could do it all over again with you—*you*, not anyone else—I would. Thank you, thank you, thank you."

Eventually my gratitude toward the child spilled over into gratitude to God, and I found myself fervently, earnestly praying. Not necessarily for my child to live, but for my child to know, before we ever parted (then or in sixty years) everything I felt for him or her, everything I was trying to say. That he or she would know me somehow, and never forget.

Turns out everything was fine. Baby kicked on, oblivious, and I went back to some semblance of a normal life. But I was different. I was newly, deeply aware that I live on the knife-edge of radical grief—that we all do, every day, every mother in the world.

Not long after that, I came across three lines from a poem by Kathleen Norris that named what I had experienced. In "Ascension" she writes,

> Now the new mother, that leaky vessel,
> begins to nurse her child,
> beginning the long good-bye.[1]

It was the phrase "the long good-bye" that hit me. It echoes what we read in today's Scripture, the prophecy that an old man named Simeon said to Mary the mother of Jesus when her son was just days old. It could be today, it could be decades from now, but you will say good-bye to your child. Someday I will lose my mother, or my mother will lose me.

Someday the same will happen with my son. This is what you sign up for in motherhood: the long good-bye. It may come sooner; we pray it will come later. But it will come someday.

And that's the heartbreak. That's where every mother knows something the greatest theologian in the world could never explain—something Mary knew to the depths of her bones—which is that suffering is part of this thing called love, and the parent suffers along with the child. And we have a God who knows this rending from the inside out.

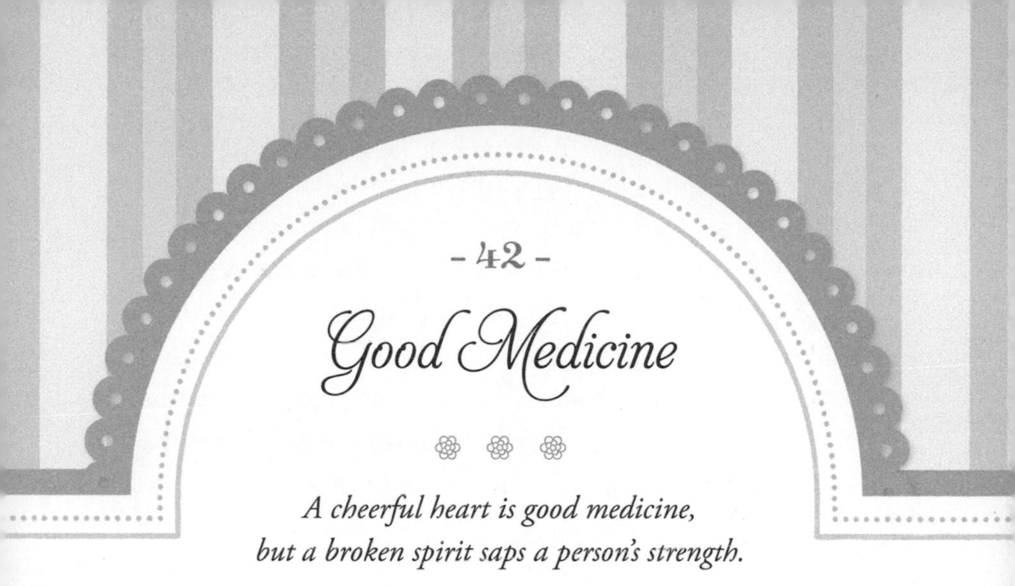

- 42 -

Good Medicine

A cheerful heart is good medicine,
but a broken spirit saps a person's strength.

PROVERBS 17:22

JUST WHEN I'M BEGINNING to feel like motherhood is a long journey through a dark tunnel of sad thoughts, soul-crushing fears, and general depression, my son smiles for the first time. It happens while his father is walking him around the house, trying to calm his fussiness by creating various distractions. At one point Tom places Micah in the crook of his arm, facing outward, and spins a little wooden carousel of zoo animals that someone made for a baby shower gift. Suddenly a ripple of delight crosses Micah's face, then a crooked little smile, pulling up first one corner of his mouth, then the other. His gaze drifts to me standing in the doorway, trying to catch the moment on video, and he smiles again.

We melt. Well, I melt, and Tom the Stoic gives a little chuckle. Later, while the baby sleeps, I watch the video over and over again, laughing out loud. It's such a contrast to how I've been feeling lately—my body painful and sluggish in its recovery; my arms and back tired of carrying the baby; my mind a blank; my emotions a wreck—that I nearly weep with relief. We're over the worst of it, thank God. I can begin the climb up and out, back into some semblance of a normal life. All because my baby smiled.

An old friend gave me some helpful advice right before Micah was born. I had just walked down the aisle in another friend's wedding (yes, I was the biggest bridesmaid ever), and we were enjoying the music and festivities at the reception, when she turned to me and said, "After the baby is born you will cry all the time. It's totally normal to cry every day, multiple times a day, for the first two weeks at least. But if it goes on longer—if, after two months, you're still crying every day—don't be ashamed to get help. There's medicine for that."

It was good, wise advice. Six weeks into motherhood, I'm not crying every day, but I'm not myself, either. And for many women, the journey gets darker before it gets lighter. Hormones wreak havoc with an otherwise balanced personality, making you wonder if you'll ever find joy in the world again. Small tasks seem overwhelming. Even caring for your baby, which you know should give you deep delight, takes every ounce of energy you have—plus all the ounces you don't.

As my wise friend said, there's medicine for that. God is not ashamed of our sadness and has put people here to help. We are not flunking motherhood if we call our friends or small-group leaders, our pastors, doctors, or therapists to say, "I'm still sad." Don't go it alone.

And meanwhile we can be grateful that God has timed our baby's first smile right when he knows we need it.

- 43 -

Asking for Help

Commit everything you do to the LORD.
Trust him, and he will help you.

PSALM 37:5

IN THE PAST FEW DAYS it has become clear that while I am climbing up and out of a postpartum funk, my husband is not. He is very frank and open about this. When the baby is fussing and nothing seems to help, and my husband takes a pacifier and throws it as hard as he can at the door, we know that something more than sleep deprivation is going on. There's a low-grade rage that terrifies him, that makes him worried he will hurt the baby. And I worry that he's worried, while at the same time feeling frustrated that I now appear to be raising two children, not one.

He goes online and discovers—wouldn't you know—there is such a thing as paternal postpartum depression. There's actually an online test dads can take to determine if they're suffering from PPD and should get help. Tom takes the test, confirming what we had already begun to suspect, and then bursts into tears. And then he calls a therapist to set up an appointment.

He's been telling his small group from church about his struggles, asking for prayer. And—wouldn't you know—every single dad sitting around the table says, "Oh, I remember those days. I went through the same thing." They go on to tell stories about their anger and frustration, their feelings of sadness and helplessness, when their children were infants. Just getting it out in the open seems to take hundred-pound weights off my husband's shoulders. The guys assure him that the feelings are normal, that very few fathers actually hurt their children, that it will pass. He laughs and cries and prays with those guys, and he feels like things have finally turned a corner for the better.

Meanwhile, I'm hesitant to talk about it with anyone except my doctor. I share cautiously with a friend, and she confirms that the same thing happened to her husband when their boys were babies. "All this time we thought society was mistreating women by forcing them to stay at home while the men went out and hunted or worked," she muses. "But maybe it was the women who said, 'Get out of here and do something productive before you hurt someone.'" We laugh but then grow pensive, knowing that for a sad number of households around the world, fathers don't get help, and some of them take it out on their families.

For our small household, anyway, the mere act of naming the problem is a step toward healing. Saying it out loud to each other, to our friends, to our church family (Tom will talk about it in his sermon this week), and to professionals who can help has been vital. Committing the whole thing to the Lord rather than stuffing it down, as the psalmist says in today's Scripture, opens the door for God's healing.

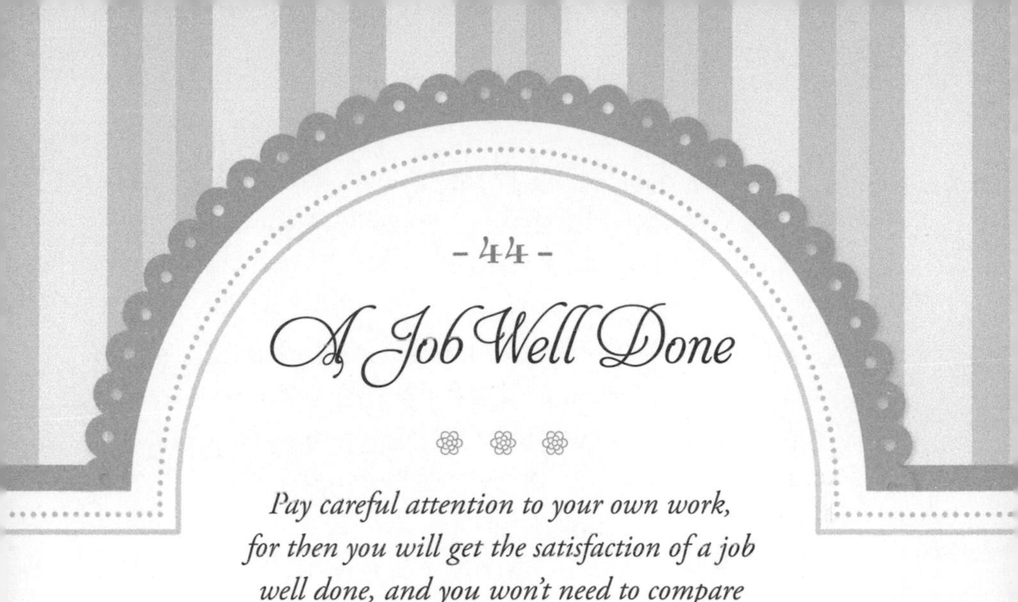

- 44 -

A Job Well Done

Pay careful attention to your own work, for then you will get the satisfaction of a job well done, and you won't need to compare yourself to anyone else.

GALATIANS 6:4

LIKE MANY PARENTS, my husband and I joined a birth class about two months before Micah was born. It was an intimate group—roughly six couples—and at first we weren't sure how well we would connect with everyone. But after the first week, it became clear that even though we came from different backgrounds, careers, and interests, we all had some important things in common: (a) we were doing this pregnancy thing for the first time, and (b) we were scared out of our minds.

We also shared a similar sense of humor, which covered up the fear and made it easier to manage. In fact, we enjoyed each other's company so much that those who could began meeting for dinner before class. At one restaurant the waitress looked at the line of four pregnant women and their partners coming in the door and said, "How many?" to which one of the dads replied, "Twelve, technically." A mom added, "*Seating* for eight, *food* for twelve."

We have since connected through online social networking, tracking the last few weeks of pregnancy and celebrating as, one after another, our babies were born. We've shared baby pictures, baby names, baby details, and now baby milestones as our little ones smile for the first time.

After a few weeks of online correspondence, someone has finally suggested a moms' night out, with the dads and babies all gathering at our house for a "playdate." Granted, the babies are only six weeks old, give or take a week, so there is more sleeping than playing. And the moms aren't able to stay out long before we begin to get antsy, wondering how the guys are doing and needing to feed our children. But it's great to gather as new parents to share our joys and frustrations, to tell our birth stories (all of them horrendous), and to line our babies up together on the couch for pictures (cutest ever).

As enjoyable as it is, I must admit: I'm more aware than ever of my inherent competitiveness. The little girl cooed already? *Oh, well, Micah was born early, so everything takes him longer.* One of the boys is only nine-ish pounds? *Yeah, Micah's a tank: we expect him to play rugby.* Another sleeps for five-hour stretches? *I wish Micah would do that!* I say none of this out loud, of course, but my brain is continually calculating the differences, making comparisons, wondering if I'm falling behind as a mom.

It's ridiculous, of course, and I can't help thinking after

everyone leaves that if I'm going to keep any friends, I need to get over myself. Motherhood is work; and, as today's Scripture says, I need to focus on the work in front of me, not worry about what other people are doing. Otherwise I will never have the satisfaction of a job well done.

-45-

Good Enough

No one is holy like the LORD!
There is no one besides you;
there is no Rock like our God.

I SAMUEL 2:2

AS I MENTIONED in the previous devo, "A Job Well Done," our birth class friends have a great sense of humor. Earlier this week one of the dads posted online, "I've figured out how to get our son to stop crying: just turn off the monitor!" Then today one of the moms posted a picture of her husband wearing a T-shirt that says "World's #4 Dad." I laughed out loud. Not number one—let's be honest here—but at least in the top five. That's awesome.

It reminds me of something I once heard from a child psychologist. Flying in the face of so much parental hype about health and safety and grooming your kids for success before they graduate from preschool, some therapists have suggested that all a child needs in order to turn out okay is "good-enough parenting." Not perfect parenting, not number-one parenting, but simply *good enough*. Show your child affection, don't abuse him or her, and, by and large, things will turn out okay.

This is a hard idea to swallow, especially for those of us brought up in a culture of overachievement. One parenting magazine I read suggested researching preschools *now*, while your child is tiny, to make sure you don't miss getting on the waiting list. Seriously? My kid hasn't even cut his first tooth, and I'm supposed to be signing him up for enrichment classes and reading to him in Portuguese? I'm supposed to surround him with organic cotton and wipe his gums after every feeding and sanitize every single bottle, every single time? What if I don't do those things? Does that put me in some special class of bad parent? Will my child turn out horribly deformed, or at least hopelessly behind the rest?

Not likely.

The biblical truth is, no human parent could ever be number one. That's God's job. God is the ultimate Father. He is the only one who can truly meet my child's needs, help my child flourish, and give my child "a future and a hope" (see Jeremiah 29:11). We could search the whole universe and there would be, in the words of Hannah from 1 Samuel 2:2, "no Rock like our God."

So you're not number one. You make mistakes sometimes. Big deal. Your child will most likely turn out okay. In fact, he or she will probably think you're number one anyway—well, most of the time. Like the restaurant I once passed that said "Voted Best Pizza by the People Who Voted," it's not the experts we're concerned about. It's the locals, the people who actually do the voting: in this case, our kids. You are the parent God has given them, and you will do your best with whatever skills and graces you have. The rest is up to the World's #1 Dad.

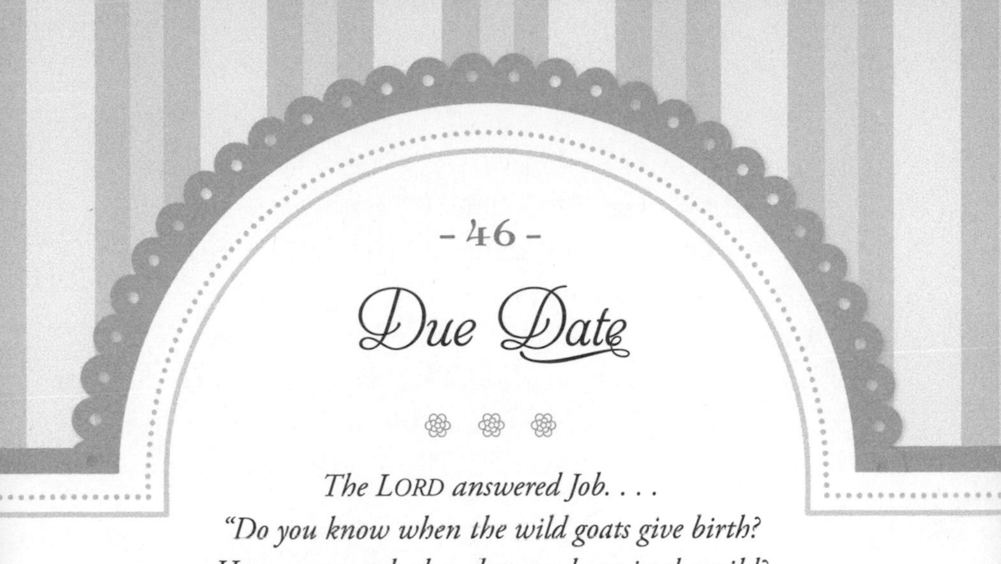

- 46 -

Due Date

The LORD answered Job. . . .
"Do you know when the wild goats give birth?
Have you watched as deer are born in the wild?
Do you know how many months they carry their young?
Are you aware of the time of their delivery?"

JOB 38:1; 39:1-2

AS I'VE ALREADY MENTIONED, my son was born three weeks early, just after Thanksgiving. It might have been the pie, or maybe the turkey. More likely it was the wedding I was in the previous weekend. Something about dashing around downtown Chicago in strappy heels, trying to keep up with the rest of the wedding party, set off a chain reaction that eventually led to the infant lying next to me right now.

I'd like to say that it was all perfect timing, that if Micah had come on his due date it would have been more difficult for our schedule or whatever. But, no, he came after the craziest month in my pastor-husband's career, with no time to relax in between. He came only ten days after I turned in the final edits for my last book, which meant I hadn't yet caught up on e-mail or housework or any of the other things that get put off till I meet a deadline. He came in the midst of a busy holiday weekend, before I'd even unpacked from the wedding, piles of laundry everywhere.

Christians like to quip that God's timing is perfect. I've certainly experienced the truth of that more than once: the encouraging call from a friend just when I needed it; the check in the mail right when the bank account was alarmingly low.

But there have been other times when God's timing has been baffling, to say the least. Like the October when a young father in our church unexpectedly died while our congregation was still reeling from 9/11—just a few weeks before I was planning to announce my final year as the church's youth director. Or the time during our seminary years that a housemate needed twenty-four-hour care following surgery just as we headed into final exams. In some seasons of life, things only get worse before they get better.

All of which point out the simple fact that I'm not in charge. Sure, it may have been our "decision" to have a baby (as if such things are within our power to begin with), but the timing of our pregnancy was something of a surprise. We may have had a kind of due date in mind for when to get serious about being grown-ups and when to start a family (after grad school, please), but nothing trumps the heavenly calendar.

The biblical character Job found this out pretty quickly when he began to ask, "Why?" (Why have all these things happened? What's God up to?) Eventually God came on the scene, responding to Job's questions with questions of his own. What did Job know about the world? What did Job know about God's timing (see today's Scripture)? Not much, Job eventually admitted. The only thing Job knew for certain was that God is God.

There's a weird kind of comfort in that. I may not understand God's timing, but neither do I have to hold the world together, carry a human life in the palm of my hand, sustain galaxies. If God can manage all that, he can manage my son's arrival. Now if he could just turn his attention to my son's sleeping habits. . . .

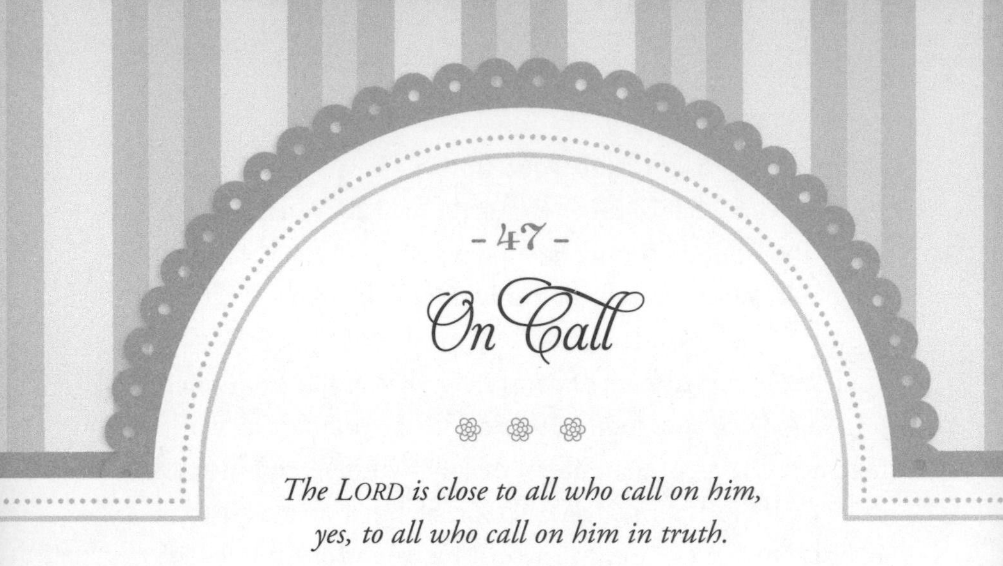

– 47 –

On Call

The LORD is close to all who call on him,
yes, to all who call on him in truth.

PSALM 145:18

I WENT INTO LABOR around midnight on Thanksgiving—or, at least that's when I realized, "Okay, this is it." I stayed in bed for a while, snoozing between contractions, hoping they would ease off like all the other practice runs I'd had already. (I was the queen of Braxton-Hicks contractions.) But they didn't go away. So eventually I got up and fixed myself a pile of Thanksgiving leftovers and ate standing at the counter, pausing periodically to let a contraction barrel through me like a train.

After a few hours I decided I should probably call my doctor. She's a member of our church and a good friend besides. But by this time it was three thirty in the morning, and Friday is her day off. I put off calling her as long as possible, worried that this was going to ruin her family holiday or send her grumbling to the coffeepot to complain with her colleagues.

But instead a perky voice answered, "Hi!" To my surprise her phone buzzed with background noise like she was at a Big Ten football game.

"It's me. Sarah."

"I know! You're calling me at three forty-five in the morning. That means you're in labor."

"Why, yes, I am," I replied, grinning. "Did I wake you up?"

"Oh, no!" she said—and then to someone else, "Grab those shorts. The ones on that rack." Then into the phone, "No, we're at Kohl's."

"You're . . . ?" I was speechless.

"You know, for Black Friday. All the stores opened at midnight. We've already been to Target."

I began to laugh. "You mean, you're not sleeping in on your day off?"

"Are you kidding? (Honey, get that other shirt—yeah, the blue one.) Actually, I'm on call. But it looks like I'll be delivering a baby."

And she did—although, not for another thirty hours. By that time she was wishing she had ditched Kohl's and slept through the night, and I was wishing I'd eaten more Thanksgiving turkey while I'd had the chance. But somehow we got through it.

I learned something from my doctor that day. And it wasn't just all the medical stuff, like the official term for when a baby's head is crooked in the birth canal. (Trust me, I could have done without that one.) Rather, it was about the character of God.

I've already said that we can't wake God up because God

never sleeps. And I've celebrated God's unwearying, relentless love. But that frosty Friday morning my doctor reminded me that we can't surprise God. There's nothing I can throw his way that will startle him, shake him up, send him into a panic. As Psalm 145:18 says, he is already close to us. He's always on call.

So why am I always surprised when he answers?

- 48 -

"I Love You, But . . ."

The mountains may move
and the hills disappear,
but even then my faithful love
for you will remain.

ISAIAH 54:10

I DON'T REMEMBER much that was said or done during labor, but there's one line I will never forget. It was when my doctor—our friend and fellow church member—was getting ready to perform some kind of procedure to check what was going on down there. As she prepared to stick her hand up you know where, she looked at me with a mixture of sadness and compassion and said, "I love you, but I have to hurt you." And without waiting for a response, she moved in.

It hurt, just as she'd promised. I think I even hollered a thing or two. But something about her words kept me from despairing. She wasn't doing it as some kind of punishment because I deserved to suffer, or because she hated the sight of me. It was because pain was part of the process of bringing about something good. The fact that she was involved in—and even, in some sense, the source of—the pain did not change the simple truth that she loved me.

She had demonstrated her love in many ways already. She had just confirmed it out loud. And now came a moment when love did not feel like love. But it was.

I will do the same for my son someday. In fact, I already have. I have given medical staff permission to poke him, wash him, weigh him. I have stripped off his warm clothes in order to change his diaper, chilly air shocking his tiny body. I have strapped him in his car seat, taken his temperature, cleaned the wound that would become his belly button. Someday I may have to do worse things, things I don't even want to think about. All because I love him.

The same is true in our relationship with God. God has demonstrated his love for us time and time again: the gift of a new day, the kind words of a friend, air in our lungs, food on the table, a sunset that fades to a color no eye before has seen. And God has repeatedly articulated that love throughout the Scriptures. Lamentations 3:22 says, "The faithful love of the LORD never ends!" and Romans 8:39 asserts that *nothing* can separate us from the love of God in Christ Jesus.

But sometimes God looks at us with a mixture of sadness and compassion and says, "I love you, but this will hurt." Today's verse affirms that all kinds of crazy things may happen, but "even then [God's] faithful love for you will remain" (Isaiah 54:10). In order for some good thing to happen, love might feel a lot like pain. We may not understand it; we may not like it—even God does not delight in our suffering. And, I should add, not all suffering is a direct act of God for some greater good: some of it is just life, and some of it is the result of evil. But we do not despair, because we are held in the hands of one who loves us.

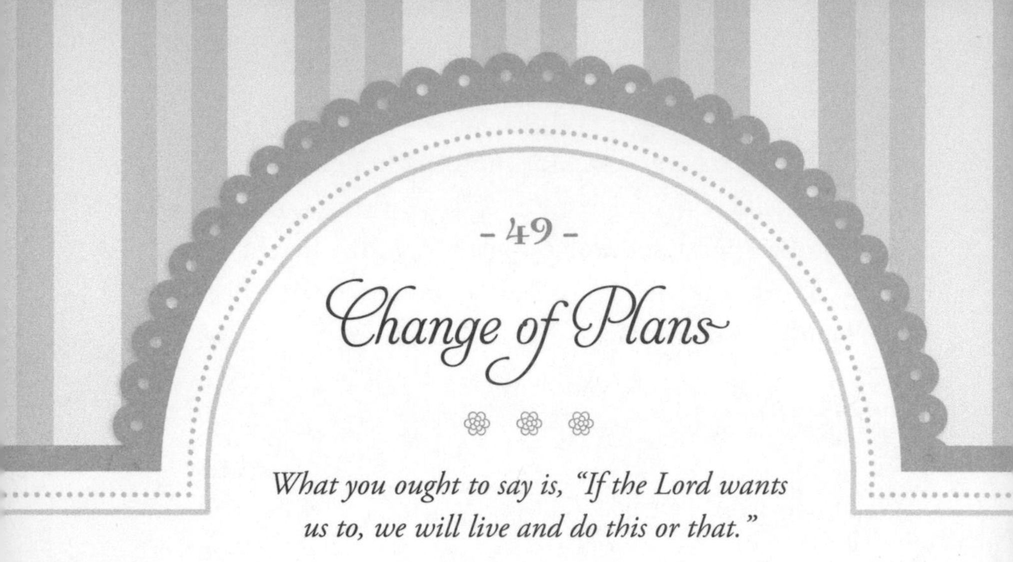

- 49 -

Change of Plans

What you ought to say is, "If the Lord wants us to, we will live and do this or that."

JAMES 4:15

I REMEMBER THE MOMENT it became clear I would have to have a C-section. It was some ungodly hour of the morning. We were exhausted, unwashed, starving, emotionally spent. My husband and I held each other and cried. We had given it our best shot, and now it was time for Plan B.

Well, this was actually Plan W, by that point, but who was keeping track anymore? Weeks earlier, prompted by our birth class instructor, we had written a birth plan, followed by numerous edited drafts. It was short and simple. We wanted a natural birth as much as the hospital setting would allow. We were to be consulted about every decision, especially if it involved some kind of medical intervention. No meds, please. That was Plan A.

Things went fairly well for the first, oh, twelve hours. Our doctor and the rest of the team were on board, and all our preparations guided us well. But then it came time to push. And push. And push some more. Baby was not moving. We broke the water: still no baby. At some point I had pushed so long and hard that we had to back off. And that's when Plans B–V came about, one after the other, every trick of the medical trade anyone could think of. But Baby would not come out.

Eventually the experts concluded the baby's head was crooked in the birth canal, which meant no one was going anywhere. The c-word was suggested. Everyone grew quiet. Since the baby was doing fine, my husband and I asked for a moment to ourselves.

As I said, we cried. We shared our anxieties. We said "I love you" forty-seven hundred times. And then I began to weep—not just cry—*weep*. "I just want to see my baby," I sobbed. "I just want to hold my baby in my arms." End of discussion. Tom went and got the team, and Plan WXYZ began.

Sure, it wasn't what we had hoped for. The birth plan had been nice: it had provided good guidance for a while, but then life pitched us a changeup. And in the end, things turned out okay. Maybe not ideal, but okay.

Isn't that the way it goes? Not just in labor but in life? I may have my mental plan about where things are headed and how they're supposed to go, but the vast number of unknowns is beyond my ability to grasp. And that's just from a scientific perspective. From a spiritual perspective, God will do whatever God feels is best—and he's not always going to alert us ahead of time. As the New Testament suggests in James 4:15-17, we may *say* we're going someplace to do something or other, but the fact is, we only accomplish those things if God gives the okay.

So it's fine to have a birth plan, or a life plan, or whatever. But in the end it's up to God.

(And now, God willing, my baby will sleep so I can fix a sandwich.)

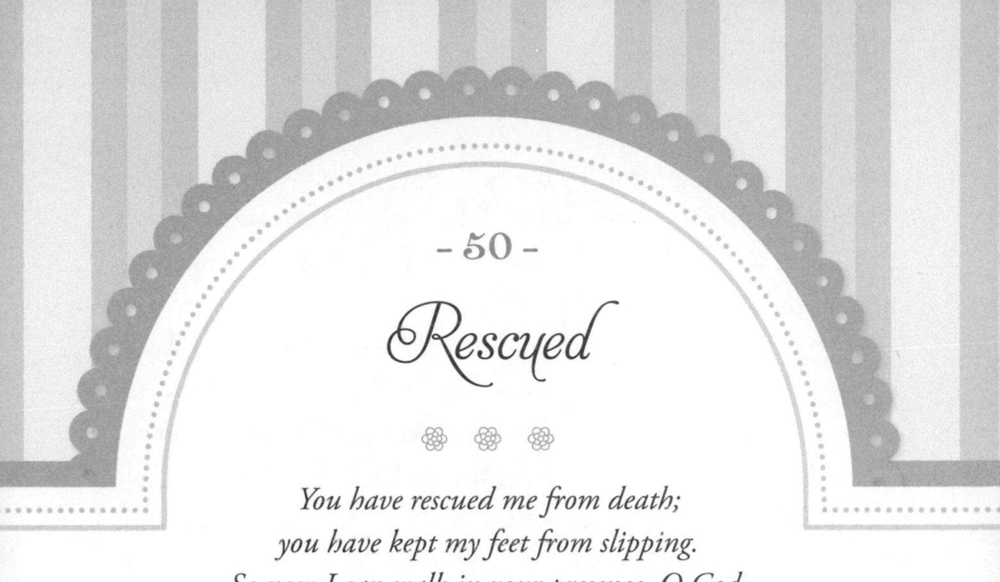

- 50 -

Rescued

You have rescued me from death;
you have kept my feet from slipping.
So now I can walk in your presence, O God,
in your life-giving light.

PSALM 56:13

THE REALITY OF MY SON'S difficult delivery is just now setting in. The first month or so I haven't had much time to be reflective: I've mostly been scrambling to keep up, happy to grab a snack and a three-hour stretch of sleep while I can. Now we've begun to hit our stride, a kind of rhythm that allows me to think about other things. And for whatever reason, my mind turns to the crazy adventure our bodies have just been on, how difficult and torturous the whole thing was, how the outcome could have been tragically different. My only response is a kind of terrified awe: terror at the fact that no matter how modern our medicine is, birth is still hard and awe at the fact that by God's grace, *through* modern medicine, my son and I are here at all.

A couple of years ago I did some research on one of my favorite writers, Jane Austen, the early nineteenth-century British authoress of *Pride and Prejudice*. I learned how, during that time period, a woman's friends would come to visit her in the last few months of her pregnancy. Ostensibly it was to "keep her company" when she could no longer go out in public. But in reality it was to say good-bye. Nobody acknowledged this out loud, but the truth was that many women died in childbirth. Pregnancy, while exciting, probably also felt like a death sentence. So a pregnant woman's friend would come over to her house, sit drinking tea and chatting about baby clothes and baby names, and then rise to leave, wondering if it would be the last time she ever saw her friend alive.

If I lived in 1817—or in a Third World country today—my husband would now be a childless widower. I might have been able to push the baby out, despite his crazy position, but the inner damage could have been catastrophic to me, and he might not have survived the trauma. That kiss my father gave me as I got into the car, laboring hard, might have been the last one. The sight of my mother's face, smiling through tears, might have been my last glimpse of her. My husband's hands and voice might have been the last things I knew in this life. And my child . . . I can't even think of my child.

Labor and delivery are hard. They are the closest I have ever consciously come to death. The fact that I'm alive at all, as Psalm 56:13 says, is because God rescued me from dying. He used my doctor and a host of medical professionals to intervene on my behalf, saving me and my baby. What other response is there except humble gratitude?

- 51 -

Here to Serve

Even the Son of Man came not to be served but to serve others.

MATTHEW 20:28

IF MY HUSBAND and I learned anything in our birth class, it was that we didn't have the faintest clue what we were doing. At one point our instructor said something like, "And if all of this seems overwhelming, you can always hire a doula."

My husband's ears perked up. "A what?"

"A doula. Someone who is a trained birthing coach, an attendant who will be with you through the whole process. . . ."

I'm sure the instructor said a lot more about it, but my husband had heard enough. On the drive home we decided that—short of stealing—we would beg or borrow what it took to hire . . . whatever that person is called . . . a *doula*. Someone who has assisted at dozens of births, who has a wealth of knowledge about labor, who could provide support and insight when we were too tired or emotionally distraught to think or act for ourselves. I could see the heavy loads of anxiety lifting off my husband's shoulders.

A faint memory stirred in the back of my brain. *Doula.* Why did that word sound so familiar? And then I remembered. Ah, yes. From studying New Testament Greek. The word *doulos* means "servant," or more properly, "bond-servant" or "slave."[1] Jesus often used the word *doulos* in his parables[2] as a metaphor for the relationship between God and God's people—not in the sense of a master who treats his servants harshly, but as a way to describe the kind of devotion we, God's servants, should have for the will of God. Jesus even told his disciples in Matthew 20:27-28, "Whoever wants to be first among you must become your slave [*doulos*]. For even the Son of Man came not to be served but to serve others." Seems like a strong word—*slave*—doesn't it?

Yet even the apostle Paul uses it throughout his New Testament letters to describe how we are no longer slaves to sin but slaves to righteousness (see Romans 6:19). More than once he refers to himself and other ministers as "bond-servants"[3]—not mindless drones, working away at endless drudgery in appalling conditions, considered less than human, but more like, well, doulas. Helpers, companions, cheerleaders. Invited to be part of the really important stuff, the really amazing stuff, the stuff that actually matters. Attending the great work that Jesus is birthing in others.

So in that sense we are all doulas, I suppose. What a tremendous privilege!

- 52 -

Arranging the Details

We can make our plans,
but the LORD *determines our steps.*

PROVERBS 16:9

ONCE WE DECIDED we needed a doula, then came the trickier task of actually finding one. My husband surfed the Net, eventually identifying a few locals who might work. Now all we had to do was interview them.

The first woman on our list sounded pretty cool: a young Christian, mother of a toddler, training to become a midwife. But more important, she had a special ministry as a doula for homeless women. In fact, she took the paying jobs like ours in order to support her ministry. That in itself made us want to hire her. I got all misty eyed thinking about our child being helped into the world by such hands, hands that had held those of the poor, the outcast, the broken in the moment of their greatest need. But she insisted on an interview, saying she wanted to be sure we were comfortable with her.

We agreed to meet at a coffee shop. For some reason my husband and I were nervous as we pulled into the parking lot. It felt like a blind date. We were about to meet someone who eventually would see us at our worst: emotional, exhausted, unwashed, and (in my case) unclothed. There was no telling, in the midst of labor, as to what words, noises, accusations, or even obscenities would come out of my mouth. Would she like us enough to stick it out? And then I remembered: oh yeah, we would be paying her to do that. Not to like us, necessarily, but to stick it out.

As we got out of the car, we realized we were parked next to some folks from our church. We greeted them, exchanged chitchat, then mentioned we were there to interview a doula, expecting to have to explain what the word meant. Immediately one of them said, "Oh yeah! I know a great doula. She's a family friend. If this one doesn't work out, I can give you her contact information. Her name is Connie."

My husband and I exchanged a glance. Connie was exactly the person we were there to meet. If the homeless ministry thing wasn't a sign, then the weird coincidence in the parking lot surely was.

I know God does this every day, arranging details. No matter what our needs, big or small, he fulfills them, according to his plan, with seemingly little effort. We may have our own plans, but as Proverbs 16:9 says, "the Lord determines our steps." What feels like a huge and daunting task to us is no great shakes to him: a simple shift in schedule, a slight adjustment in timing, a nudge that moves in one direction or another.

So why am I always surprised when it happens?

- 53 -

Right There with Us

The LORD your God . . . will neither fail you nor abandon you.

DEUTERONOMY 31:6

DESPITE THE FACT that I was ready to hire our doula the moment we read about her online, we agreed to meet her for an interview at a coffee shop. After the parking lot coincidence (see the previous reading, "Arranging the Details"), I was ready to tell her, as soon as she walked through the door, "God wants you to be our doula. You just don't know it yet."

Instead I looked up, up, up at the solid, capable woman who greeted us, and I resisted the urge to give her a humongous hug. That's the only kind of hug it would be possible to give and receive with Connie. She must share the same gene pool as Paul Bunyan. Her hands could split and stack firewood with ease. Each arm is decorated with tattoos, including a whole set depicting the stages of fetal development. On at least one occasion I have known her to wear a black T-shirt that says, in plain white letters, PUSH.

Yet somehow, in spite of all this, she is not intimidating. You want to hug her. Or at least, I wanted to hug her. Our doula, live and in person, there to the rescue.

Instead we shook hands politely, smiled and exchanged various greetings, and then sat and talked. I am not kidding when I say that it was less like an interview and more like my husband and I trying to convince her that we were cool enough to be her friends. She smiled and nodded and asked questions, but even when it was all over she said, "Well, think about it and pray about it, and we can follow up when you decide."

We knew this was wise, that we should probably meet with a few other doulas, just to be sure. But deep down in my heart, it was settled. I would have Paul Bunyan's granddaughter, or I would have no one.

I knew God would be with us at the hospital. Even if we didn't have a stellar team of medical professionals, God would not leave us for one moment. (We *did* end up with a stellar team.) But there was something about the thought of Connie, tall and strong, holding my small hands in her powerful ones, that made the presence of God very real. When the Bible says in Deuteronomy 31:6 that God "will neither fail you nor abandon you," I don't think it's a purely spiritual promise. I think God surrounds us in the midst of our pain and struggles, not with mere promises, but with people. His people. People like Connie.

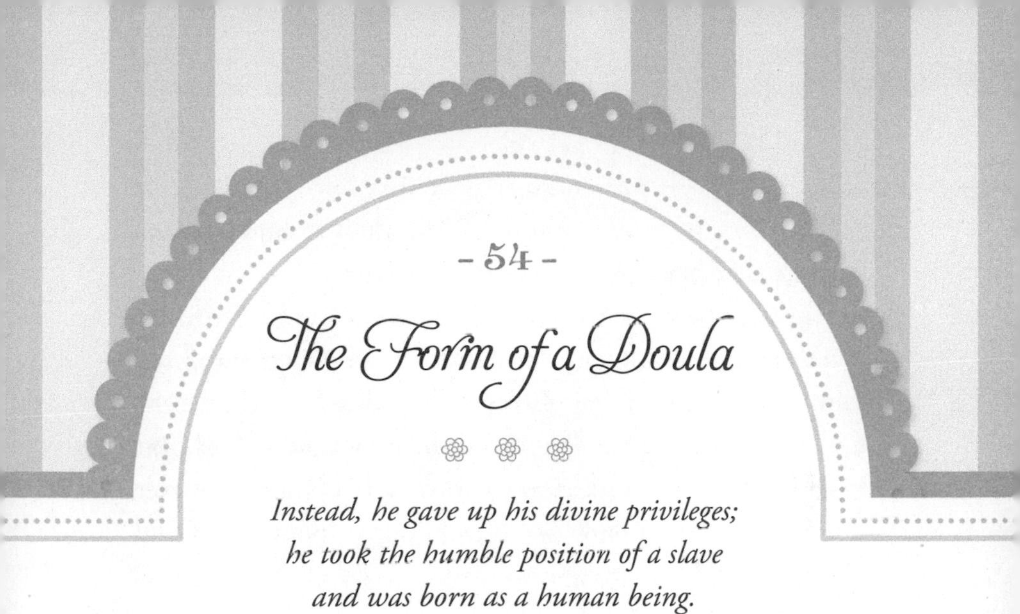

- 54 -

The Form of a Doula

Instead, he gave up his divine privileges;
he took the humble position of a slave
and was born as a human being.

PHILIPPIANS 2:7

AS IT TURNS OUT, we didn't have the chance to interview any other doulas (see pp. 139–142). Early on Black Friday I went into labor, three weeks before my due date. I made two phone calls at four in the morning: first to my doctor, and then to Connie. We hadn't yet confirmed her as our doula, hadn't signed the contract or even sent in a deposit. But she picked up after a few rings, sleepy and slightly amused.

"Hi, Connie?" I said. "Do you still want to be our doula?"

She began to chuckle. "Let me guess. You're in labor."

"Yep. I know we didn't sign a contract or anything—"

More laughter. "Don't worry about it. Tell me what's happening, and we'll go from there."

I told her, and we went from there. Straight to the hospital, in fact. First for assessment in triage, where she shielded my view from the monitor so I wouldn't become obsessed with what was happening on the screen; and then to labor and delivery, where she quickly got to know more about the Arthurs than anyone ever should.

She paced and rocked with us, conferred and laughed with our doctor, respectfully deferred to the nurses on duty, and calmly suggested different positions or techniques. Her strong hands held mine, pressed on my back, held up an index finger in front of my face and commanded, "This is your birthday candle: blow it out! Blow!" At one point she told my husband to go eat and then later to lie down and nap—and he did so, gratefully, like a compliant child.

In short, we did whatever Connie told us to do. If anything, you might have thought the traditional master-servant roles—usually associated with the Greek word *doulos*, meaning "slave" (see "Here to Serve," pp. 137–138)—were reversed. And yet she didn't leave us for a moment.

One of the oldest Christian hymns, Philippians 2:6-7, celebrates the servant humility of Christ:

> *Though he was God,*
> *he did not think of equality with God*
> *as something to cling to.*
> *Instead, he gave up his divine privileges;*
> *he took the humble position of a slave*
> *and was born as a human being.*

There's that word again, right in the second-to-last line: "he took the humble position [*form* in the NRSV] of a *doulos*"—which, as Connie demonstrated, is not the same as a doormat. Like a doula, Jesus is on call at all hours, walks with us through the difficult times, tells us what to do when we're overwhelmed, and takes care of our needs with the expert mastery of a professional caregiver. He never leaves our side.

Maybe that's why, whenever I hear that Scripture now, I picture Jesus in a T-shirt. A black one like Connie's. The one that says PUSH.

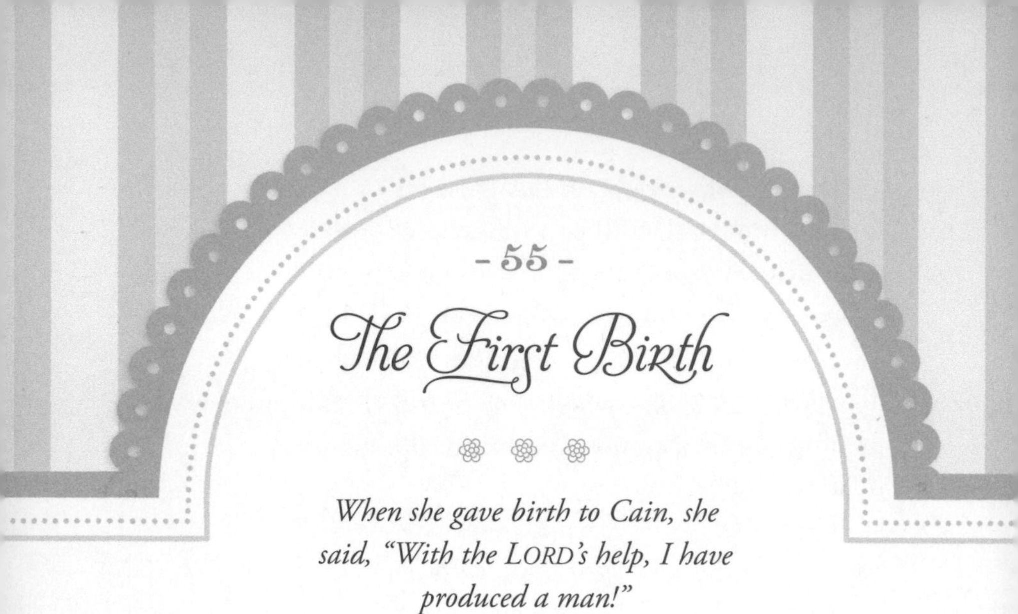

- 55 -
The First Birth

When she gave birth to Cain, she said, "With the LORD's help, I have produced a man!"

GENESIS 4:1

I SOMETIMES WONDER what it must have been like for the first woman ever to give birth. I picture Eve, round with what must have seemed like a crazy alien tumor, bent over in the grip of hideous pain. The grip releases, she straightens, walks a few steps, wonders whatever happened to her husband. At least the pain is gone. But then, no, there it is again, like a snaky vine tightening relentlessly around her belly. She bellows Adam's name, staggers to the cave. There's no mother or mother-in-law to hold her hand, no doula to call. The pain returns, over and over, with no one there to reassure her it won't last forever, no generations of women to share their advice.

Adam hears her, makes a dash for the cave. Water, blood, sweat, his wife in agony. She is in labor, he realizes. He has seen other creatures give birth—has attended at the births of lambs and calves—but never before has he witnessed such a battle. He remembers the words God spoke before he and his wife were banished from the Garden, the promise that Eve would bear her children with intense pain and suffering (see Genesis 3:16). And yet Adam never imagined it would be like this. Surely he must lose her. But no: hours later, a great rending, and then a squalling creature emerges, the world's first-ever human baby.

Trembling, Eve takes the child, exhausted. And then she says a curious thing: "With the LORD's help, I have produced a man!" Not, "with Adam's help." Not, "*Adam* and I have produced a man." Just Eve and God. No acknowledgment that Adam had any part to play in the child's conception, nor that he's even there at all. (I'm simply exercising my imagination when I suggest he was there, since Scripture doesn't say.) Despite the fact that her difficult labor, according to Scripture, is the direct consequence of her disobedience in the Garden, she recognizes that God has been involved from start to finish.

If there's anyone in the history of humankind who had reason to think God would take zero interest in her survival, it would be Eve. She had turned her back on him, after all, disobeying God's direct command and encouraging her husband to do the same (see Genesis 3:1-6). God had pronounced what their respective punishments would be and then banished them from the place where all their needs were met, where they were in deep communion with God and each other (see Genesis 3:23). Any of us, in the same situation, would assume that God doesn't care anymore: we're on our own. Good luck.

But that's not what Eve seems to think. God is intimately involved in the birth of her son. And not just involved, but *helping*. She may have sinned, but that doesn't cut her off from the grace and intervention of her heavenly Father.

If that is true for Eve, then isn't it true for us?

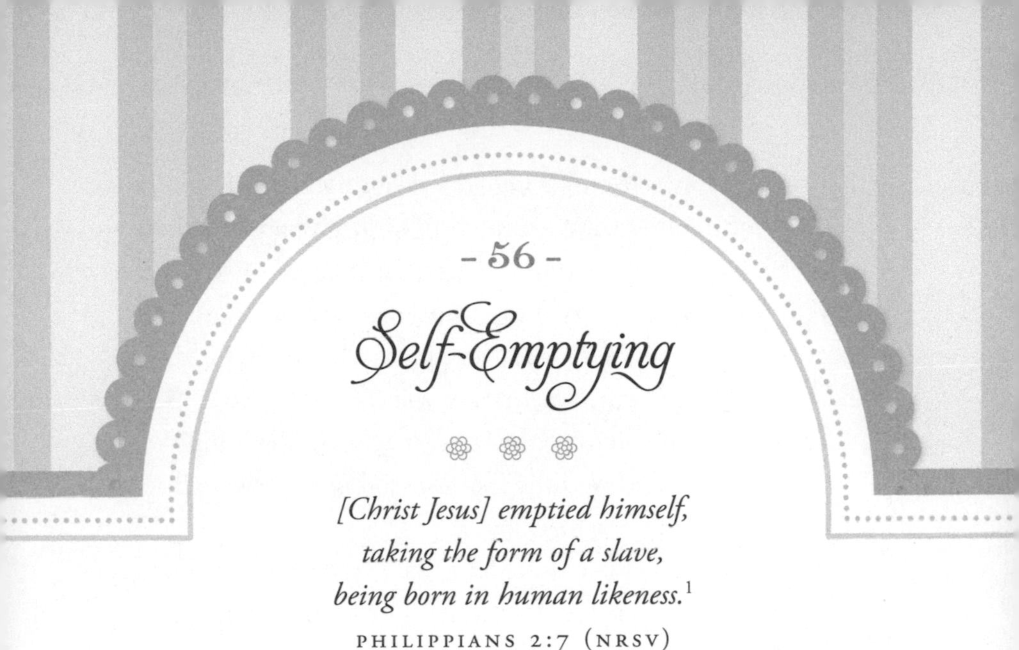

- 56 -

Self-Emptying

[Christ Jesus] emptied himself,
taking the form of a slave,
being born in human likeness.[1]

PHILIPPIANS 2:7 (NRSV)

I'VE DESCRIBED MY WHOLE LABOR story already (see pp. 126–134), so I won't repeat it here, but suffice it to say we wouldn't have broken my water unless it was really important. And the moment we did, I felt a gush of relief unlike anything I've felt before or since. Months of weight and pressure and discomfort poured out in what felt like a waterfall. It seemed to last forever, like I would look down when it was all over and my body would have deflated like a balloon. I had emptied myself.

Of course, there were still many pounds of baby and other stuff to deal with, so the relief didn't last very long. But in the moment I had the strange feeling that I was somehow pouring myself out—and not in a negative way. Like it was possible, out of my fullness, to empty myself without losing any essential part of who I am. This is what I wanted to do, this release, this self-emptying, because much good would be the result, even if things got worse for a while before they got better.

I'm using that term "self-emptying" on purpose, of course. It's an echo of today's Scripture, which comes from an early Christian hymn celebrating what Jesus did for us (see Philippians 2:5-11, NRSV). Christ, who is God, was willing to "empty himself" and become like us, willing to serve and to die.

Yet theologians for many long years have debated what that phrase "empty himself" means. Does it mean he gave up his divinity? His power? His divine knowledge? His glory? But without those things, how could he have conquered disease and sin and death? Or have had the wisdom to perceive what was in people's hearts? Or remained pure and sinless? Or had moments when his glory was revealed, as in the Transfiguration (see Luke 9:28-36)? Could God empty himself of anything without becoming less than he was before?

I suspect that moms might be able to answer that question. Because nothing empties you like labor and delivery. Nothing empties you like caring for an infant. You pour yourself out—literally and figuratively—all day and all night, even when you're supposed to be sleeping. You release, out of the fullness of yourself, all the loving energy that you ever thought you could hold, and then you do it all over again the next day.

You empty yourself, but not in a way that diminishes you, as if you are now less of a person than you were before. You empty yourself in order to fill another, and in the emptying you are revealed in all your strength for who you really are. This is your true character, this pouring out. You are not losing yourself, or even any part of yourself. This is who you have been from the beginning. Now you are simply sharing it with another, whose life and flourishing would not happen without you.

So step aside, theologians: let the mothers of the world show you how it's done.

- 57 -

Unclean?

You must obey all my regulations and be careful to obey my decrees, for I am the LORD your God. If you obey my decrees and my regulations, you will find life through them. I am the LORD.

LEVITICUS 18:4-5

IN THE ANCIENT RELIGIOUS customs of the Old Testament, women were considered "unclean" after childbirth.[1] The word *unclean* applied to all kinds of situations: illness, infection, menstruation, dead bodies—whenever there was blood or decay or other human waste involved. It was not just a statement about sanitation, as in "Ew, that's gross; don't touch that." It was a religious statement, a statement about the body's spiritual condition. If you were "unclean," you had to go through a period of waiting in which other people were not to touch you, and then you had to perform all kinds of purification rituals—washing and praying and offering sacrifices—and then the religious leaders pronounced you "clean."[2]

Women, it seems, got the bad end of the deal. Menstruation alone meant that at least once a month, you were "unclean" and had to separate yourself from regular society.[3] After pregnancy and delivery, you were unclean for a while—anywhere from a week to two months, depending on how the purification laws were interpreted. Because you had come so close to death and had shed so much blood, it would be a while before your normal life could resume.

Now, some folks today read those passages and assume that the culture of the time was heavily prejudiced against women. The more women could be shut out of regular society, the less power they had and the more men could be in control. But after going through childbirth myself, I have begun to wonder: what if those laws were put in place, on a subversive level, to *protect* women?

In the ancient world, a woman was considered the property of her husband. And a man could do whatever he wanted with his own property—even sleep with her right after childbirth if he wanted to—right? Not so fast. This woman, this creation of God's, needs time to heal. She needs space to connect with the baby, a window of rest in which to take a break from the demands of life for a while. You touch her, you're breaking God's rules.

I can just picture Moses passing along the instructions about purification, and all the men saying, "Wait: I don't get to touch her for *how long*?" and all the women saying, "Hallelujah! Make it longer!" The men could grumble all they wanted: God had laid down the law.

Today, most people (with the exception of some Jews,

depending on their form of Judaism) don't strictly follow the purification rules. When it comes to childbirth, we take our cues from the medical world, which suggests not lighting the fires of romance for at least six weeks. But I'm thinking the Old Testament is on to something. Not that I don't love my husband and want to be with him. Not that I don't appreciate his kind touch, the warm hug, the occasional massage. But something significant has happened to my body—and not just medically speaking.

I have drawn near to death. I have looked into the abyss. I have come, in some indefinable way, closer to God. I need a moment to pause, to consider, to rest. In this hallowed space, set apart for a time, I belong to God first.

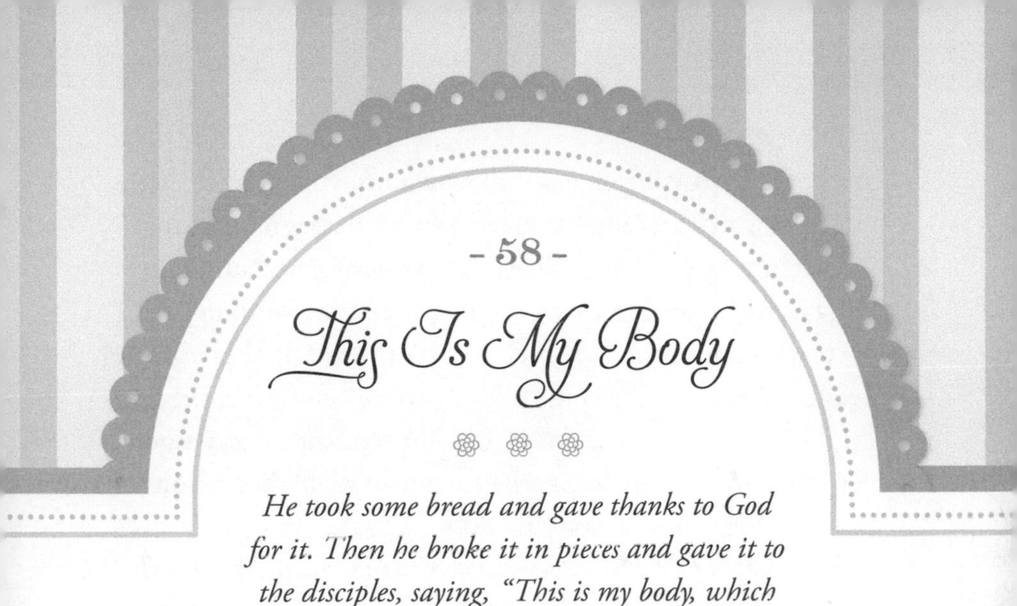

- 58 -

This Is My Body

He took some bread and gave thanks to God for it. Then he broke it in pieces and gave it to the disciples, saying, "This is my body, which is given for you. Do this to remember me."

LUKE 22:19

I WAS TALKING with some other new moms lately, and in addition to our various woes about time and sleep, a common theme was "I want my body back." Even if we weren't nursing, we were still adjusting to the postpregnancy alterations our bodies had gone through: the widened rib cages, the slightly larger feet, the extra layers of cushion all around. "I pee every time I laugh," said one mom—at which point we all laughed, because we all know what she means. And then one by one we excused ourselves to the bathroom.

My body—what does that mean, anyway? After pregnancy, I'm not so sure. This human frame, which I thought I knew so well, went through radical changes and experienced radical events that I had zero control over. There was another living being inside of me, sending cues that had nothing to do with my own rhythms of eating and sleeping. (How many nights, as I was falling asleep, did my baby decide my internal organs were a trampoline?) Now that my baby is here, I rarely get to sleep or eat or wash myself in the manner that I choose, *when* I choose. Is this body really mine?

This strikes me as a difficult and even fearful question for women. For millennia, the female body has been considered the property of men who rank higher on the social scale, whether fathers, husbands, or older brothers—even masters, kings, or lords. Simply by virtue of their superior strength, men have sometimes considered women's bodies available for the taking, whether they had permission or not. Only after many decades of women taking a stand and saying, "This is *my* body," have these deeply rooted assumptions been challenged and changed in some parts of the world.

But spiritually the issue is far more complex. On one level, yes, this is my body. And nobody—not even my husband or child—has any inherent claim on it, to take what they want without my permission, as if I'm their property. Yet, at the same time, my body is not really my own. It is mine only in the sense that God has given it to me to take care of—specifically, to use for his glory in serving others.

Social and political engines may encourage us to insist on our personal rights, that these are our bodies to do with what we choose. Yet those same engines are not prepared for the woman who says, "I choose to give my body for others." And, to be quite honest, I'm not sure I'm ready to be that woman. But it's a step in the right direction to acknowledge that the only person who really can say, "This is my body," is Jesus. If his example is anything, that means the body is a gift to be given. Yikes.

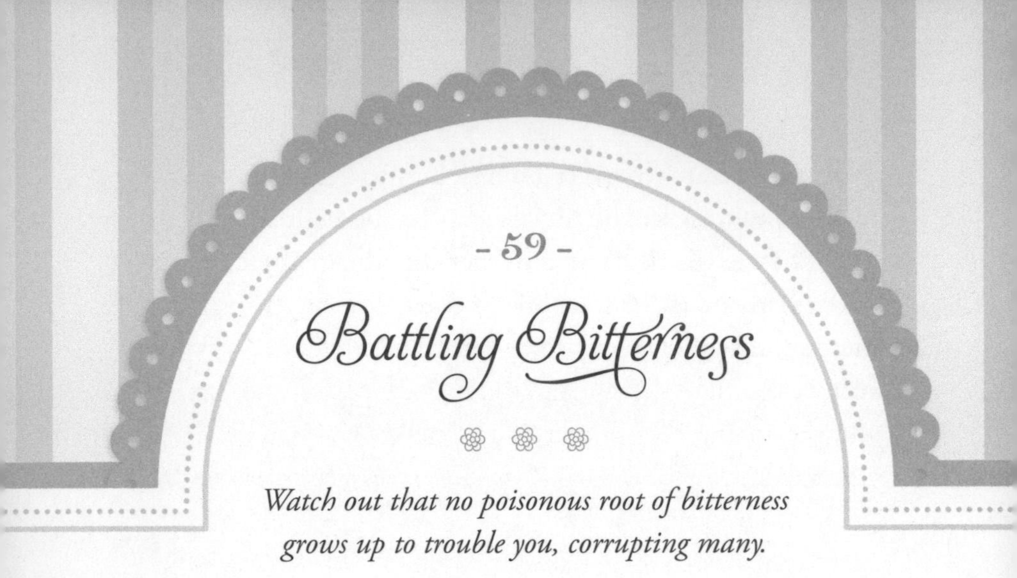

– 59 –

Battling Bitterness

Watch out that no poisonous root of bitterness grows up to trouble you, corrupting many.

HEBREWS 12:15

APPARENTLY THE WHOLE QUESTION of whether or not a mother's body is really hers (see "Unclean?" and "This Is My Body," pp. 152–157) does not disappear as a baby gets older. One mother describes how, for some reason, her thirteen-month-old must have his feet on her at all times: when he's taking a bottle or getting a diaper change or just sitting on her lap hearing a story. He's always pressing his feet against her legs or arms or stomach, any part of her on which he can get some purchase. Even if she shrugs him off or sidles away, one little foot will wave in the air till it finds her. But it's such a silly annoyance that for a long time she didn't bother to tell anyone, including her husband.

Then one night she crawled into bed next to her husband, who snuggled up against her and then slid his feet onto hers. To the poor man's astonishment, the mom yanked her feet away and bellowed, "Get your feet off me!" Her response then took some explaining, which turned to laughter. But he hasn't put his feet on her again.

If she's anything like me, what that mom really craves is a touch-free zone. Not just the feet, but everywhere, for five minutes, maybe even an hour. If everyone could just get their sticky little fingers off me, maybe I could recover my sense of self, the feeling I'm somewhat in control of my life. All this embodiment is bad enough without having to share it with the rest of my family.

Obviously, Micah at this age has no idea that I am a separate person from him. In his little world, I'm just an extension of himself, the larger, nonstationary part, the part that supplies comfort and nourishment. I may step out of his line of sight periodically, but then I return, like my own hand that disappears into a pocket and emerges again. He has absolutely no concept that I live a whole other life apart from him and his needs, that I think my own thoughts or fold laundry while he's sleeping or want to cry sometimes myself.

I know it won't last forever. But in the meantime it's exhausting to be someone else's planet. And if it isn't my son, it's my husband, needing, needing, needing. It's hard not to be bitter sometimes.

I know I shouldn't be. I want to be able to offer myself to my family as a free gift because it is my joy to do so. I want to be able to say, as Jesus did, "This is my body, given for you." But the giving is not easy, as Jesus well knew. It requires taking up a cross and pain and sacrifice. It requires daily battling the bitterness that threatens to poison me, as today's Scripture suggests. I must keep watch and not let that root grow.

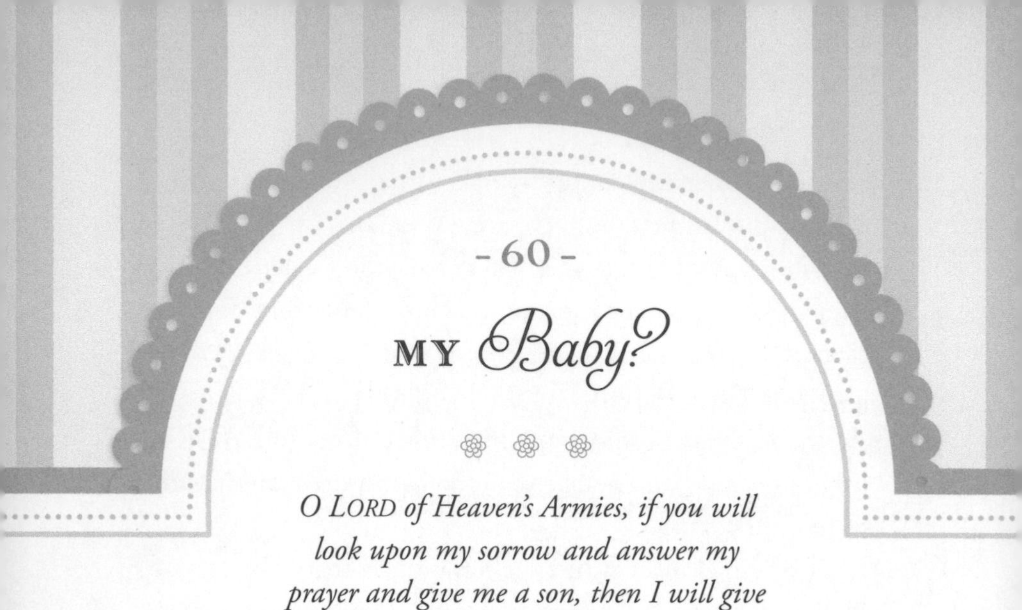

- 60 -

MY *Baby?*

O LORD of Heaven's Armies, if you will look upon my sorrow and answer my prayer and give me a son, then I will give him back to you.

I SAMUEL 1:11

IN THE MIDST of exploring whether or not my body is really mine (see pp. 152–159), I've begun to wonder if the same question extends to the way I think of my son. It's the word *my* that's tripping me up. Yes, I gave birth to this child. He is—biologically, legally, and most every possible way—mine. And yet, as I said in the very first devo, everything I know about my Christian faith tells me that he isn't. He belongs to God.

But, oh, how I've dug in my claws! If someone else has been holding him for too long, I want him back. My arms ache for his little body. My eyes study his every feature, poring over the details as if I made him from scratch myself. It is unfathomable that this child could be anything other than mine.

That's why today's Scripture is so challenging. Here was this childless woman, Hannah, whose intense longing for a son caused her to pray so fervently in the Tabernacle that she was mistaken for a drunk (see 1 Samuel 1:9-18). Her prayer was so earnest that the priest, Eli, blessed her. She gave birth to a child whom she named Samuel, which Hebrew scholars suggest sounds like the term for "asked of God." Hannah herself said, "I asked the Lord for him" (1 Samuel 1:20). Sounds like a permanent gift to me.

But Hannah wasn't making an empty promise when she told God that if he gave her a son, she would give the boy back (see today's Scripture). As soon as the child was weaned, she brought him to the Tabernacle and told the priest Eli, "Now I am giving him to the Lord, and he will belong to the Lord his whole life" (1 Samuel 1:28). It wasn't merely a euphemism for raising him to know God, like the dedications of infants that some churches do today. No, the Bible says in 1 Samuel 2:11 that after a beautiful song of praise, Hannah and her husband "returned home . . . without Samuel."

Without Samuel. She fed him one last time, wiped his hands and mouth, told him to be a good boy. She held him for a long moment, kissed the curls on the back of his neck, felt the warmth of his body against hers. And then she turned and walked away. She had made a promise, and she meant it.

As impossible as Hannah's choice seems to me, she was only living out, in concrete detail, a spiritual reality that already exists. I know that Micah is God's creation, given to us as a gift for this short time. Not only that, but Jesus redeemed Micah from sin through his death and resurrection: so if there's anyone who rightfully "owns" him, it's Jesus. And someday, when this life is over, I pray Micah will return to the one who made him and saved him. Not even in heaven will Micah be mine.

So Hannah's choice faces me, too, just on a different level. It's the daily unclenching of the fist, the letting go.

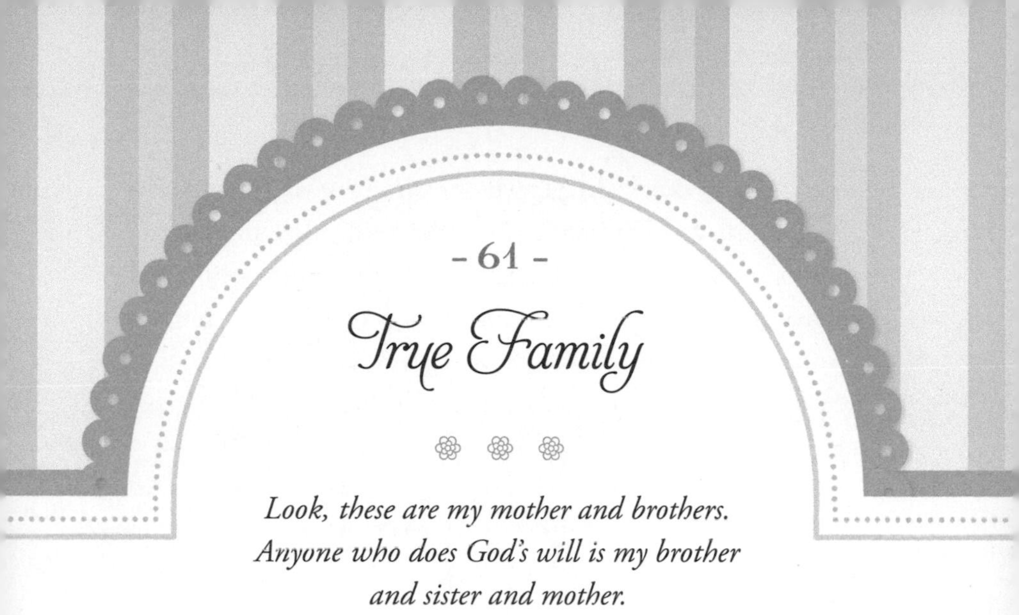

- 61 -

True Family

Look, these are my mother and brothers.
Anyone who does God's will is my brother
and sister and mother.

MARK 3:34-35

THE BIBLE HAS THIS DISCONCERTING habit of messing with our notions of family. There's Hannah, who gives her long-awaited son back to the Lord—and as I discussed in the previous devo, not just metaphorically, but literally, to be raised by the priest Eli in the Tabernacle. And then there's Jesus himself, who, when told that his mother and brothers are waiting for him outside, turns to those around him and says *this* is his family, those who seek to obey God (see today's Scripture). Elsewhere he goes so far as to say, "If you want to be my disciple, you must hate everyone else by comparison—your father and mother, wife and children, brothers and sisters—yes, even your own life" (Luke 14:26). Needless to say, these passages are not usually top choices for worship services on Mother's Day.

But the early Christians took them quite literally. Take the story of two young martyrs who died in Carthage during the third century, for instance. The story goes that these brave women—one an aristocrat named Perpetua, and the other a slave named Felicity—were imprisoned with a number of other Christians for refusing to renounce their faith. The crazy part? Perpetua was a nursing mother, and Felicity was eight months pregnant.

Perpetua writes in her own words about how much she suffered until finally her baby, weak with hunger, was brought to her in prison so she could nurse him. Then she writes, "I grew strong and was relieved from distress and anxiety about my infant; and the dungeon became to me as it were a palace, so that I preferred being there to being elsewhere."[1] Perpetua was a mom like everyone else. Just give me my baby, for pity's sake. Everywhere is a prison without him.

Needless to say, Perpetua's nonbelieving father did everything in his power to get her to renounce Jesus. He pleaded, he commanded, he begged her to have pity on his old age and consider how the child would die without her. But Perpetua would not budge. Later, at the trial, her father was beaten in front of her; and then he took her son and would not give him back. Even though she begged for the child, she would not be moved. It was only by God's grace, Perpetua writes, that from that point her child no longer needed to nurse, and she herself healed quickly, without fever.

Felicity's story is also incredible, but I'll save that for the next devo. Suffice it to say, the trial ended with Perpetua and her companions being sentenced to execution: death by wild beasts in a gladiator arena. They were hauled away to the dungeons to await the day of the games, rejoicing that they were considered worthy enough to suffer for the sake of Jesus Christ.

What is family, by this definition? I hardly dare to think. It's something radical, something that goes beyond the bonds of blood and clan. I can only imagine that, because of Perpetua's example, her son was able to make a stand himself one day. And then mother and son would have met on the other side of death, knowing they were family in the only way that matters.

Could I do the same?

- 62 -
Crowd of Witnesses

Since we are surrounded by such a huge crowd of witnesses to the life of faith, let us strip off every weight that slows us down, especially the sin that so easily trips us up. And let us run with endurance the race God has set before us.

HEBREWS 12:1

IN THE PREVIOUS DEVO, "True Family," I talked about the Christian martyr Perpetua, a nursing mom who was imprisoned and sentenced to death for refusing to deny her faith in Jesus. Along with her was another young woman, a slave named Felicity who was eight months pregnant. As I hinted, her story is incredible.

Felicity wasn't afraid of death. She knew it was the penalty for refusing to bow to the gods of the Roman Empire. She knew we all have to die sometime, and she wanted to die a death worthy of Christ's own suffering—what the early Christians called a "second baptism" of martyrdom. When you became a Christian, you were baptized in water; when you became a martyr, you were baptized in blood. You didn't go out and seek it. You didn't make a spectacle of yourself. But neither did you hide. When the authorities came to make arrests, you submitted peacefully, all the while sharing with them the truth about Jesus.

No, it wasn't dying that Felicity feared. It was dying alone. Pregnant women were not allowed to be thrown to the beasts; so unless she gave birth soon, she would remain while her friends died in the gladiator games without her. That did not exempt her from execution later, but it would be alongside criminals rather than her fellow believers. She was afraid of giving up her last breath among strangers.

So the other believers started praying—and not that she would be spared. They prayed that she would be delivered of her baby so she could join her friends rather than die alone. They prayed so earnestly that she went into labor, even though her baby wasn't yet full term. She gave birth to a girl, there in the prison, only three days before the games. The child was given to a sister, and Felicity, along with Perpetua and the rest, faced the beasts.

Eight months pregnant and in prison. Knowing you will not raise your child. Giving birth in agony, without medication, jeered at by guards who say, "If this is how you act now, what will happen when you meet the beasts?" Turning to those guards and saying, "Right now, I'm the one suffering. But on that day it will be Christ in me who suffers, because I suffer for him."[1] Three days later rising from your pallet, stumbling in chains to the arena, and then being stripped naked by your captors to stand before the raging crowds. But you are not alone. Perpetua and your Christian brothers are there, holding your hands; and Christ is in you, "the hope of glory" (Colossians 1:27, NRSV).

What trials will I face in this life? Most likely nothing this brutal. And yet every day I am dying to sin, dying to myself, dying to the maternal fears that threaten to strangle me. And every day I am surrounded by the great "crowd of witnesses"—mothers like Perpetua and Felicity—who, even now, cheer me on. So perhaps the more important question is not, what trials will I face? but how will I face them? Will my response be worthy of the mothers who have gone before?

- 63 -
Unshakable

Since we are receiving a Kingdom that is unshakable, let us be thankful and please God by worshiping him with holy fear and awe.

HEBREWS 12:28

JUST WHEN I'M BEGINNING to think I whine too much, that I'm not cut out for motherhood (much less martyrdom), yet another terrifying parenting article comes my way. This one is about consumer products that were not properly regulated, causing injury and death to children—and about the parents who have rallied, petitioned, and mobilized to make sure it never happens to another child again. And I buy into fear all over again.

I suppose I have those conscientious parents to thank for the many safety features on my son's equipment. There are age limits on his toys, letting me know about potential choking hazards; there are grave warnings on everything from his bottles to his bassinet. And tales, echoing in my ears, of children who have perished in any number of ways, because somebody didn't realize such and such was a suffocation hazard. Apparently it's my job as a parent to stand vigilant over the forces of pain and death, making sure none of them ever come near my child. If I'm not careful, I will become a paranoid mess.

And yet, the story of Perpetua and Felicity (see pp. 163–168) makes me suspect that there are some things worse than death. For those young Christian martyrs, denying Jesus Christ was worse than death. Refusing to stand in solidarity with those who suffered for his sake—that was worse too. Raising a child who knew that his mother had given in to fear, had turned her back on eternal life in exchange for this short mortal one . . . that was worse than torture, suffering, or martyrdom.

As a Christian, I know this on a theoretical level. I know that following Jesus is the only thing worth doing, in the end. It is the most important thing Micah will ever do. But when push comes to shove, am I really ready to put Jesus first? Do I really believe that there are some things more important than helping my son avoid pain, suffering, or death? When I stand before the throne of God someday, will I honestly be able to say I rejected the things of this perishing world—the fears for my child's safety, the angst for his future—in favor of giving him "a Kingdom that is unshakable" (Hebrews 12:28)?

This doesn't mean I ignore the threats to his flourishing. If I see a suffocation hazard, I will remove it. If I hear a warning about a certain brand of baby equipment, I will be wary. A focus on Micah's eternal future does not equal a casual negligence about his current well-being. Even Perpetua, awaiting death by execution in a filthy prison, knew that her nursing child needed her or he would die unnecessarily. She begged for him to be brought there, which he was—and both of their suffering was eased. And Felicity, once she had given birth, didn't just abandon the child to fate: she released her newborn girl to be raised by a sister. Faith does not exempt you from being a conscientious mom.

But it does mean that the things of this world don't shake you. Or they shouldn't. Because you stand on something unshakable.

-64-

A Passion or Deliverance?

I want you to know . . . that everything that has happened to me here has helped to spread the Good News.

PHILIPPIANS 1:12

IN THE STORY of the third-century martyr Perpetua (see pp. 163–171), there's a fascinating moment before the trial when her brother comes to see her in prison. Apparently he is a Christian, like her, but it's hard to tell from the ancient document whether or not he is imprisoned too. In any case, he wants to know if God has given her a vision of what will happen. Will this experience, he asks, be a passion or a deliverance?

Now, to our postmodern ears the word *passion* is associated with strong emotion: if I'm passionate about something, I feel strongly about it; it affects me deeply. But passion in this context goes even deeper: it comes from the Latin *passio*, which means "to suffer." When we speak of the passion of

Christ, we mean the trial he went through in the final hours of his life, his unspeakable suffering for the salvation of the world.

So when Perpetua's brother asks if this will be a passion, he's wanting to know if she will suffer and then die. For the early Christians, to undergo a passion like Christ's was one of the ways to give him glory. Suffering was not something to be strenuously avoided. Sure, you didn't necessarily go out and seek it, but like the imprisoned Paul in today's Scripture, when it came your way, you didn't run: you turned it into an opportunity to tell the world about Jesus.

But there were other ways to give God glory, and one of them was a deliverance: a moment when God provided an escape, a release, a sudden turning of the tide. It's like Peter in prison, chained to two snoozing Roman guards, suddenly feeling the chains fall off and watching the doors to the prison swing open (see Acts 12:6-11). Like a passion, a deliverance was an opportunity to give God the credit, to tell the world about Jesus.

What strikes me about Perpetua's brother's question is his certainty that whatever the outcome, God will be glorified. The world will know about Jesus whether Perpetua dies or is set free. Her captors will hear the Good News, her city will spread the story, her family—including her child someday—will know she did it all for her Lord.

This rocks my world. How many times did I pray, while pregnant, for a good delivery—and not because I wanted to give God glory, but because I was terrified of the alternative? How many times do I pray, even now, that Micah will be spared suffering—not so I can celebrate a God who delivers us, but so Micah can excel in life? How often do I hope that I will never be one of those parents who has to bury a child—because until now it has never occurred to me that while undergoing such a passion, I might be given the chance to tell others about Jesus?

Whether I face a passion or deliverance someday with this child of mine, I want to be a momma like Perpetua. Able to give God the glory, whatever happens.

- 65 -

Always Watching

You are the light of the world—like a city on a hilltop that cannot be hidden. No one lights a lamp and then puts it under a basket. Instead, a lamp is placed on a stand, where it gives light to everyone in the house. In the same way, let your good deeds shine out for all to see, so that everyone will praise your heavenly Father.

MATTHEW 5:14-16

MY MOM POINTED it out to me yesterday. "See how he watches you," she said. It had happened so gradually that I hadn't really noticed. But it's true: Micah now watches my every move. I step behind him while he's in the baby swing, and he tilts up his chin to follow me with his eyes, his forehead wrinkled with concentration. Last night we gave him a bath, and his gaze didn't leave my face for a moment, earnest and a little worried, as if he was trying to figure out from my expression if I thought baths were okay, or if he was being a good boy. He doesn't yet comprehend my absence when it happens; but he can now track my movements when I'm there.

It's sweet and a little alarming. I've already mentioned how exhausting it is to be somebody else's planet (see "Battling Bitterness," pp. 158–159). Now I get to be somebody else's moral universe. My every move, whether intentional or not, is teaching him about appropriate human interaction with the world. Does my face light up in the presence of my husband? Do I slam the phone when someone I'm speaking to makes me angry? Do I welcome strangers, help an old lady with her groceries, share my food? All of a sudden what was unconscious behavior is now under close observation.

He is too young to recognize the moral impact of what his mother does in a given day, but that won't always be the case. His recent ability to watch me will become a lifelong posture—or at least a habit that continues as long as we live in the same house. He may not always fix his gaze on my face, but he will be "watching" me: that is, observing my way of life and gauging whether or not it's the kind of life worth living. In time he will know all the little nuances of my behavior: if I'm trying very hard, for instance, to hold my tongue; or if my kind gesture to a homeless person seems natural or forced.

Hopefully by now the moral habits of the Christian life have become second nature for me. God knows I've been schooled in them so long, by so many amazing Christians who have walked this path before me, that those habits should be natural. As author C. S. Lewis once noted, the real test of our character comes in the unguarded moments, when we don't have time to calculate a response. Those are the moments when the spotlight is on us, as today's Scripture says, when the whole world (not just our baby) is watching. The question is, will my son give glory to God for what he sees?

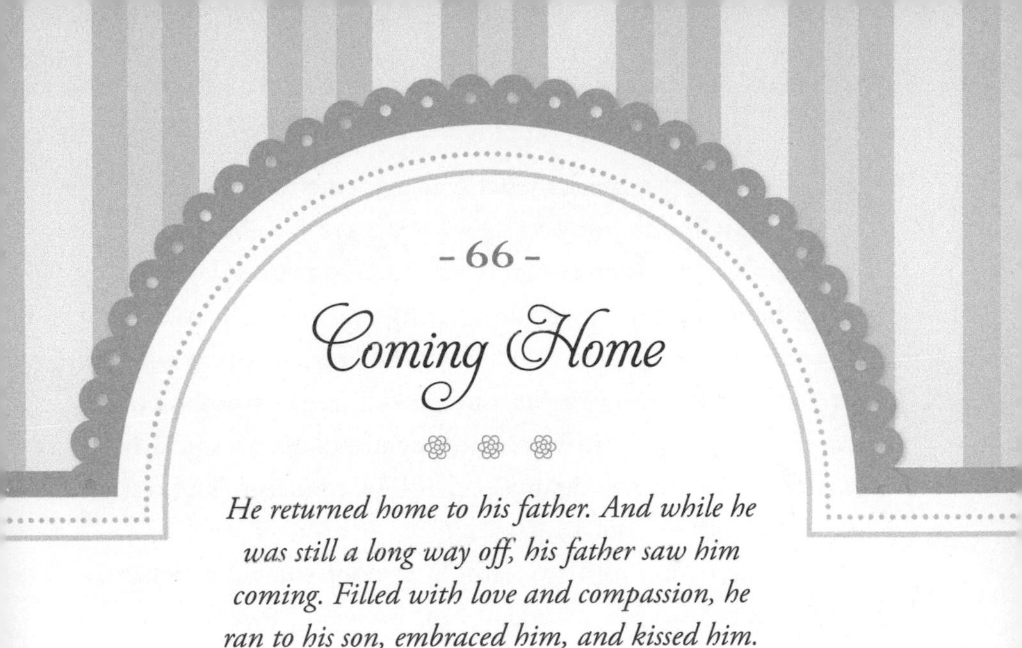

- 66 -

Coming Home

He returned home to his father. And while he was still a long way off, his father saw him coming. Filled with love and compassion, he ran to his son, embraced him, and kissed him.

LUKE 15:20

SOME DAYS I WANT so badly for my son to grow up to follow Jesus that it hurts. It's not just a vague, "Oh, I hope he's a good boy" or "I hope he's nice to people." It's a deep ache, almost like grief, mixed with a painful kind of surrender. At the end of all things, when we stand in the presence of God, there are no guarantees that Micah will join the fellowship of those who say, "Yes."

It seems silly to contemplate this now, when he's still so small. I won't go into all the complicated theories about the salvation of infants and to what extent God's grace covers us before an age of accountability. Suffice it to say, someday he will stand on his own spiritual legs, make his own moral choices, be held accountable for the things he does. He will either look in the face of Jesus and see there the love of his life, or he will turn away.

I can't make that choice for him. I can only live the story of grace in my own life, sharing it as naturally as one shares how the sun rises in the east and sets in the west. I can only make the spiritual soil as rich as possible. I can water and weed; I can watch the weather; I can pray that whatever seeds his father and I plant will flourish. The rest is up to God.

For the first time I'm getting a taste of what the father in the parable of the Prodigal Son must feel like. Today's Scripture from Luke 15 tells only a part of the story, the happy ending, if you will. But the parable begins with the son asking his father for his share of the inheritance before the father has died—in essence, saying, "I wish you were dead already." The father gives what he asks; and the son goes off to a distant land, where he squanders his money in reckless living. Finally, broke and broken, he realizes that he must go home and beg for forgiveness.

Verse 20 always gets me. I can just picture the father on the porch, shielding his eyes, studying the distant figure on the road. Is it . . . ? Yes, it must be. He would know that gait anywhere. He vaults down the steps and begins to run.

If it were your child, wouldn't you?

I would. That could be me, after all, someday. At some point my son could look at me with a sneer and say, "I wish you were dead," and I'd watch him walk out the door. He might not communicate for days, weeks, months. I'd pray and worry and hope. I'd pull out the box of his baby clothes and cry for the days when I could still hold him in my arms. And then the phone call, the e-mail, the sound of someone walking through the front door. My son coming home, back to us, back to God.

Micah may turn into a prodigal; he may not. Whatever happens, I know God will welcome him home with open arms. And if God does that for him, he does so for all of us.

- 67 -

Child of the Promise

A child is born to us,
a son is given to us.
The government will rest on his shoulders.
And he will be called:
Wonderful Counselor, Mighty God,
Everlasting Father, Prince of Peace.

ISAIAH 9:6

PARENTING ARTICLES on the Internet regularly feature ways to help your child get ahead of the game intellectually, physically, or socially. Fill your infant's room with large, colorful letters of the alphabet. Schedule playdates with parents of other ethnicities. Give your baby swim lessons. Develop your baby's palate by exposing him or her to unique international flavors. Have one parent speak another language exclusively when around the baby. And on and on it goes. . . .

At first the suggestions seem creative and even doable. Yes, when my child is old enough, I can experiment with cumin in his chicken. But after a while the cumulative effect of such tips is totally exhausting. I begin to feel, before my son is even two months old, that I am failing hopelessly as a mother. I become convinced that my son will not learn the alphabet till junior high, will never keep up with his bilingual classmates, will be unable to compete in the global market. I'm setting him up for mediocrity, all that potential for changing the world down the drain. His teachers will look at him and say, "We thought he was something special, but . . ." shrug, "not so much."

This is all ridiculous, of course. And in many ways spiritually dangerous. I am reminded of something I once heard theologian Amy Laura Hall tell a roomful of overachieving Christian high schoolers during a summer camp at a university seminary. She looked around and said, "I only get one hour to speak with you, and I want to make it count. So I asked a friend of mine, another theologian, what I should say. And he said, 'Tell them that the child of the promise already has been born.'"

The room fell completely silent.

She went on. "I know your parents have raised you to think that you are totally special and unique, that you can go out and save the world. And certainly God has formed you and has plans for your life. But the job of Savior already has been taken. You don't need success. You need Jesus."

If this was hard for a roomful of overachieving young adults to hear, I can't even imagine how their parents would have reacted. All those years of grooming their children for successful careers in medicine or law, all those cotillion classes and math camps and private tutoring, all undone in twenty seconds by a theologian who had the guts to tell the truth.

You can't save yourself. You can't save anyone else. Jesus—the child of the promise who was prophesied about in Isaiah 9 and throughout the Scriptures—already is here. And apart from him you are nothing, you can do nothing (see John 15:5).

Not easy words for us parents, but if we let them sink in, they contain the keys to freedom—both for ourselves and for our children.

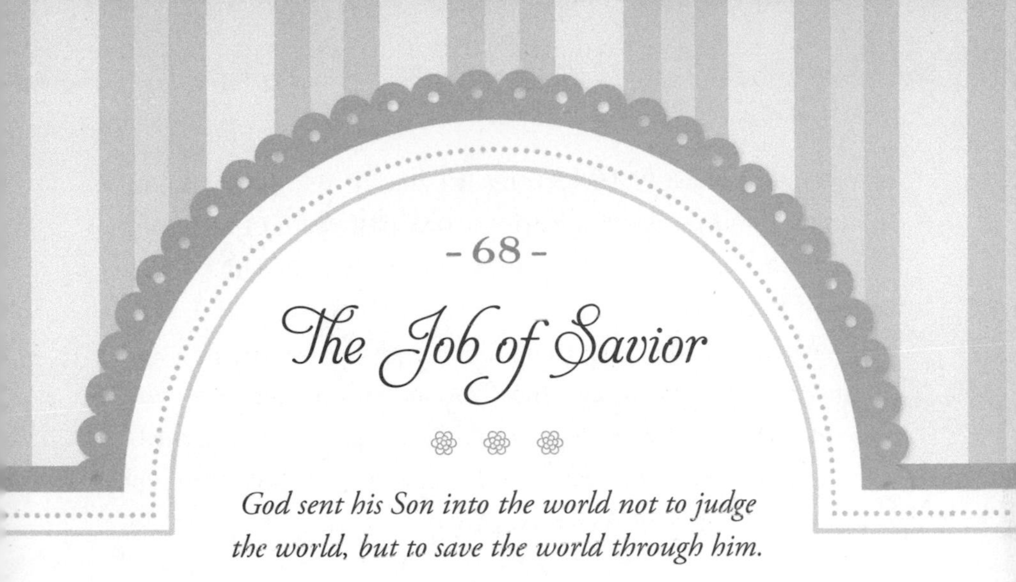

-68- The Job of Savior

God sent his Son into the world not to judge the world, but to save the world through him.

JOHN 3:17

WHEN A THEOLOGIAN told a group of high schoolers that "the job of Savior already has been taken" (see the previous devo, "Child of the Promise"), she may not have realized how convicting her words were to the adults in the room, many of whom were young parents. I wasn't a parent at the time myself, but years later, the words still ring across time and memory to land sharply in my conscience.

How many times a day do I freak out about the potential harms that may come to my newborn child? How often do I want to save him? Before I lay him down in the cradle near the fireplace, I double-check that the propane is off and inspect the vents for cold drafts. Before we go anywhere in the car, I adjust his seat belt a dozen times, making sure there are no zippers or buttons or other choking hazards in the way. All night long, if I'm not getting up for feedings, I'm checking his position, adjusting the thermostat, rewrapping his swaddle, making sure his little arms are free so he doesn't roll over accidentally.

And all of these are good, wise things for a parent to do. But it can get overwhelming if you let your imagination run wild. The number of hazards to a newborn are beyond measure. Preparing for all of them could task your last strength, and that's in addition to the normal, everyday things you do just to keep yourself and your household functioning (such as, say, eating a meal). But in the back of your mind all the time is the niggling fear that if you are not looking out for this kid, who is?

It's the same question I will ask myself when my son is a teenager, reaching for the car keys or packing for his first semester of college. All those old fears for his safety, all those desires to shield and shelter and save him from the dangers of this world, will come flooding back in force, grown stronger by the fact that he will be out of my reach. I can feel the panic rising even as I write these words: *out of my reach*. When I'm not there to help, who will be?

The answer is simple, of course. God in Christ will be there. He will be looking out for this kid. The truth is, already my child cannot take a breath apart from the sustaining grace of his Creator. I am not the one putting air in his lungs or ensuring that his heart pumps so many liters per minute. I am not the one arranging his rescue from the powers of darkness. As today's Scripture makes clear, my son's Savior is not me, after all, but Jesus Christ.

The problem is—if I'm honest with myself—I don't really trust God to take care of my son as well as I do. That, my friends, is wrong. It is a sin. I confess it, fearfully, praying for the grace to release my son into the hands of the only one who can truly save him.

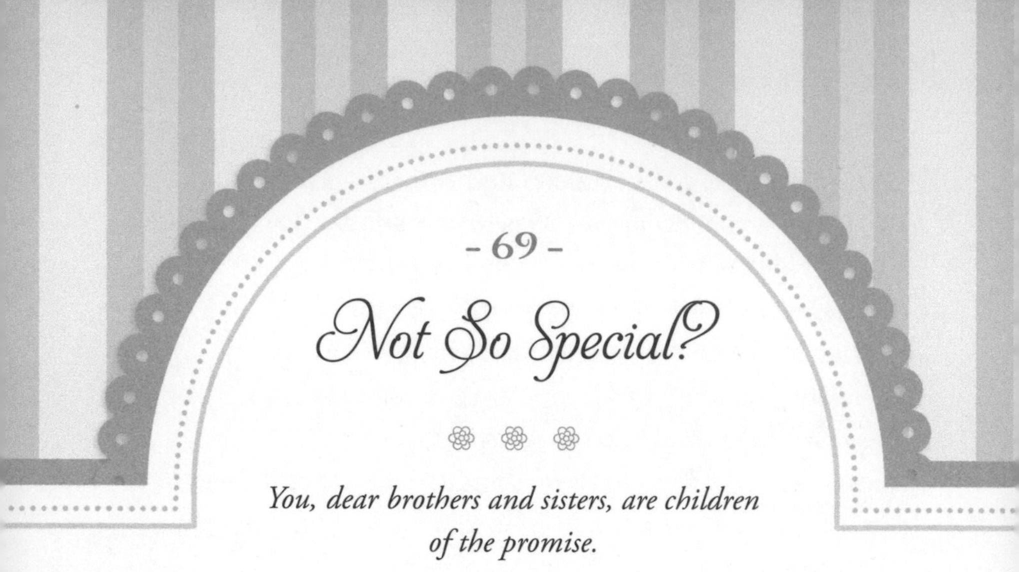

- 69 -

Not So Special?

You, dear brothers and sisters, are children of the promise.

GALATIANS 4:28

AS I DESCRIBED in a previous devo ("Child of the Promise," pp. 180–182), I once heard theologian Amy Laura Hall tell a roomful of Christian high schoolers that "the child of the promise already has been born." While on one level the kids seemed to understand her point—that Jesus is the one we put our hope in, not the next generation of overachievers—there was a rumble of protest at the idea that all their grooming for success had no value.

One kid raised his hand. "But we are special, each of us, aren't we? Everyone tells us that. Even the media tells us that."

The theologian smiled sadly and said with compassion, "Yes, you are a very important consumer market."

The kid looked at her blankly, but the adults in the room knew exactly what she was talking about. Especially the young parents, many of whom made up the staff of that particular summer program. They didn't need a theologian to tell them that kids are an important consumer market: all they had to do was look at their own monthly budgets.

It begins before our kids can even pay for anything themselves. We parents are bombarded with advertising for the latest baby gear and gadgets, pressured by well-meaning friends or family members into buying things we aren't even sure we need. Much of that pressure is built around fear: if we don't get this bottle warmer, our babies may reject their source of nourishment. If we don't get bumpers for the crib, our babies might wedge their little heads between the government-regulated rails—never mind that bumpers themselves can be a hazard. If we don't get this particular play mat, complete with bright colors and swirling shapes, our children will never develop the motor skills to learn how to sit up, much less compete in a global market.

It doesn't stop as our kids get older. Eventually they will have their own budgets, whether through allowances or work, and then as teens they will enter the largest consumer market on the planet. If there is a cult of youth in our country—if the hipsters are taking over the world—it is because most advertising and marketing is geared toward those under the age of twenty-five. They have disposable cash, which means they have power. And they have been told, from the time they were tiny, that they are special, that they can change the world. Aren't they entitled to the best?

As Christian parents we have the opportunity—nay, the mandate—to combat the colonization of our children into little consumers. Yes, they are special. But that's because they are made in the image of God, saved by the grace of Jesus Christ, and empowered by the Holy Spirit to do amazing things. They are, as the apostle Paul says in Galatians 4, "children of the promise," not because of anything extraordinary about them, *but because of Jesus*, through whom they are heirs of the covenant God made with Abraham.

That is a radically different understanding of the human person than just a wallet with legs, as the theologian well knew. That's the truth I want my son to embrace, before he ever holds a penny in his hands.

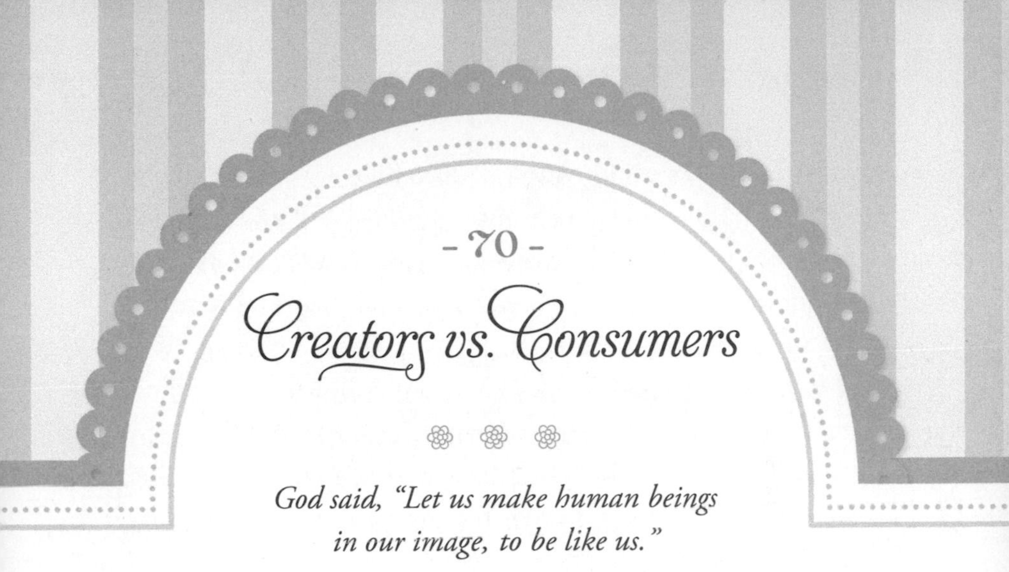

- 70 -

Creators vs. Consumers

God said, "Let us make human beings in our image, to be like us."

GENESIS 1:26

WHEN THE THEOLOGIAN told the high schoolers, "You are a very important consumer market" (see pp. 180–188), she was not trying to cut them down. She was stating a simple fact about the way our kids are viewed by the world at large. Micah, at two months old, might as well have a dollar sign on his Onesie. Given the amount of stuff required just to take him on an overnight visit to relatives, we should buy stock in a major baby gear retailer.

So how does one raise a nonconsumer? How does one raise a child who is aware that he or she is more than just the sum of her family's bank accounts? These are the questions my husband and I ask ourselves when the material frenzy gets overwhelming. Is it enough to acquire most things homemade or "pre-loved" and to request a green baby shower, complete with recyclable plates? Is it enough to ask the grandparents to contribute to a college fund for Christmas and birthdays rather than to inundate our clueless infant with more stuff?

Such gestures are a start, anyway. But I have a feeling it goes even deeper. It goes all the way down to a biblical claim about who we are as human beings. As writer Dorothy Sayers once noted in *The Mind of the Maker*, when God suggests in Genesis 1:26 that human beings are to be made in God's own image, one of the only things we know about God from the Scriptures up to that point is that God is a creator. So if humans are made in *that* image, it must mean that one of our primary characteristics—indeed, our primary calling—is to be creators too. Not creators on God's scale, able to make something from nothing, but creators on the next level down, able to take the materials and ideas that God has put in the world and fashion them into something useful or enjoyable or both.

I was blessed to have been raised by parents who wanted their children to be creators rather than consumers. It was a lifestyle they modeled themselves. Shopping was not a family pastime. My father made our first outdoor playhouse from the overturned hull of a wooden boat—using scraps he hadn't needed when restoring a sailboat several summers earlier. Meanwhile my mother sewed or knit many of our clothes. Early on my sister and I were encouraged to play outside, to draw using scrap paper, to recycle old clothes for dress-up or making costumes, and in general to see something that other people might view as waste and think, *What could I do with that?*

So when I'm tempted to buy that cute whirligig gizmo for Micah's crib, I'm reminded of my biblical and family heritage. Raising Micah to be a creator rather than a consumer starts right now: with *me.*

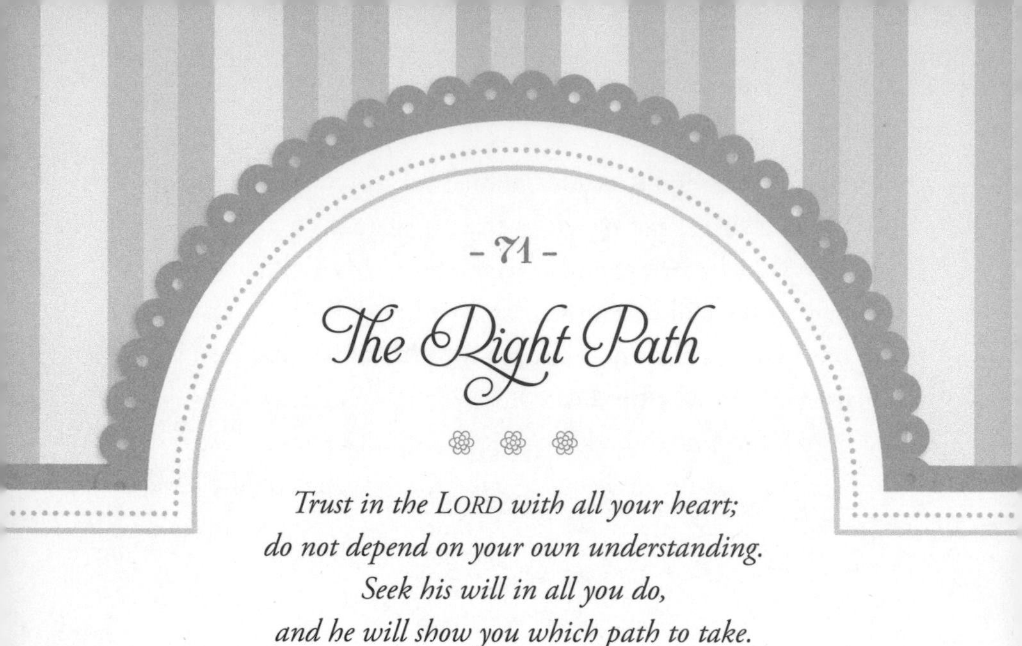

- 71 -

The Right Path

Trust in the LORD with all your heart;
do not depend on your own understanding.
Seek his will in all you do,
and he will show you which path to take.
PROVERBS 3:5-6

I DON'T KNOW if I wear this look that says, "Please give me advice about my life, my wardrobe, my haircut, my career path," or if this just happens to everyone; but I am often given unsolicited input on everything from my eyebrow hairs to my chosen vocation.

For instance, while I was a full-time youth director, pouring my heart into ministry, I met a visiting missionary who said, after five minutes, "You should be in missions! You would make a great missionary." Um, thank you? Does youth ministry seem not missional enough?

Then, after I became a freelance author and speaker (I was still a youth ministry volunteer), a new acquaintance turned to me during a conference and said, out of the blue, "You would make a great mother!" I was honored by the compliment. But did folks assume that my child-free life was somehow not fulfilling? That I wasn't giving enough of myself for other people, including the children and youth that I write for?

Perhaps my favorite example is of the older woman who insisted that when my husband went to graduate school, so should I. She herself had been highly educated in the country where she was born. She told me, in a foreign accent thick with disdain, "You can do better than *typing* for people—or whatever you do." Yes, typing for people. That sums up my vocation. That's what authors of books do.

Unfortunately, I know I've done this to other people myself. It's far too easy to make a quick assessment of someone's skills and personality and think of all the ways they could be useful to the world doing something other than what they're doing. They could land this or that job, make more money, help more people, make a great missionary or mother or med student. We're especially guilty of this when it comes to teens and young adults, as if their whole lives are blank screens on which wise grown-ups can write Op-Ed suggestions about how to live the good life.

Which does not bode well for when Micah gets older. Already people are looking at his long, sensitive fingers and wondering if he'll be a basketball player. "A cellist," I say cryptically, as if I've already seen the writing on the wall. Or maybe he'll become a mechanic, a career without which our car-dependent society can't survive.

In the end, what Micah does with his life is up to God—and whether or not Micah is seeking to follow wherever God leads. More than advising him to chase this or that career, I should pray, as the author of Proverbs says, that my son will trust in the Lord with all his heart. As much as I may want him to depend on *my* understanding, the only one he should depend on is God.

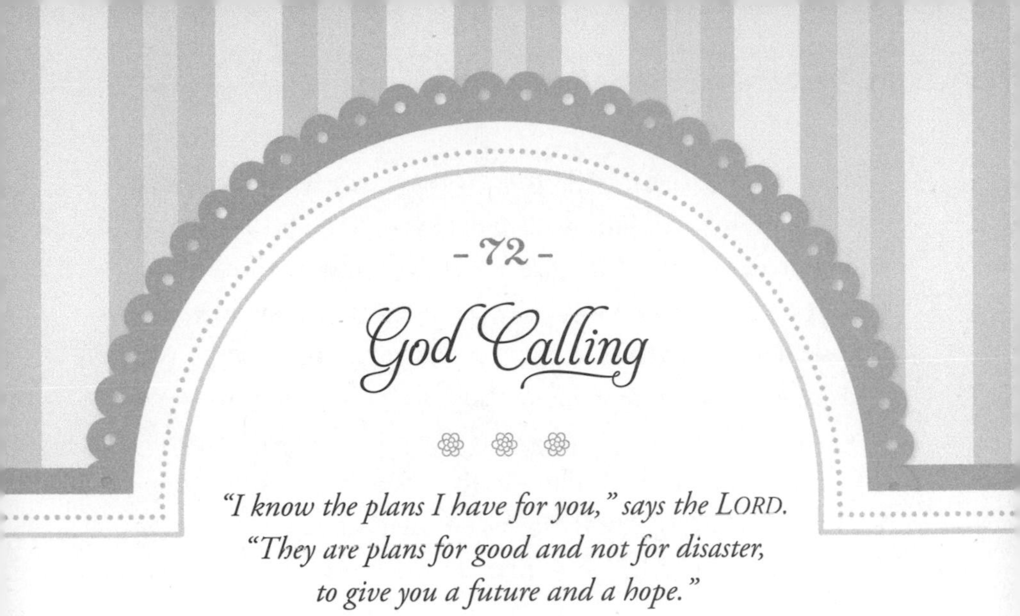

- 72 -

God Calling

"I know the plans I have for you," says the L*ORD.*
"They are plans for good and not for disaster,
to give you a future and a hope."

JEREMIAH 29:11

CHRISTIANS OFTEN TALK about hearing God's call, or pursuing their spiritual vocation, or seeking God's plan for their life. They make it sound like a person's "call" is to do just one thing, like being a missionary to Cambodia for the next forty years. It's like God put us on this earth to fulfill one big, important task that no one else can do, and until we discover what it is, we wander aimlessly, not good for much.

Motherhood has made me suspect that the issue of vocation is much more complex. Before my baby was born, I pursued the vocation of "writer," but I also wore other hats, including "theologian" (more on that later), "speaker," and "artist." Then there were the culturally defined vocations, such as "wife"—and more specifically "pastor's wife," for better or worse. Despite the demands of motherhood, I still wear some of those hats; and as my baby gets older, I'll be picking some of them back up again.

But motherhood itself is a kind of vocation. You might even say I was called to it, since it wasn't really my idea: my husband and I were pretty happy hanging out, just the two of us. Then at some point we both began to sense that God wanted us to give the family thing a try. God had a new "call" for us—although the calling itself is as old as creation (literally: see Genesis 1:28)! It didn't take long before I was wearing a new vocational hat, one that (at the moment) trumps all others.

I have to keep reminding myself that a calling is different from a job. If taking care of this infant was a job, you couldn't pay me enough to do it. Plus, I wouldn't qualify anyway: no training, no prior experience, and the only references would be from my mother, who would say glowing things about me because she's supposed to.

No, motherhood is not a job. Nor is it simply built into my DNA, like some biological drive (maybe I'm weird that way). Rather, it's a vocation. It's a calling at this specific time in my life, for some purpose that is not always clear—although Micah certainly benefits. And it isn't my only vocation. Somehow it meshes with the other roles I've been playing, the other callings I've heard over the course of my life.

Maybe that's why God says in Jeremiah 29:11, "I know the plans I have for you"—*plans*, plural—not *plan*. More than one, and often overlapping. Which is a good thing. Because when Micah is grown and leaves home, if I have no other vocation besides motherhood, what will I do with myself?

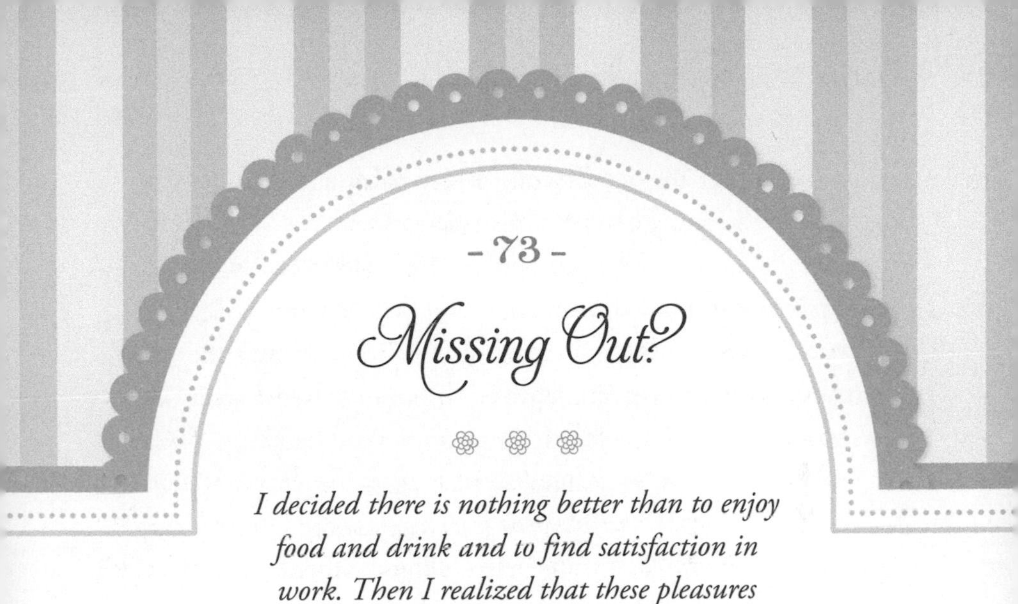

- 73 -

Missing Out?

I decided there is nothing better than to enjoy food and drink and to find satisfaction in work. Then I realized that these pleasures are from the hand of God.

ECCLESIASTES 2:24

LESS THAN A YEAR before we got pregnant, I completed a master's degree, with honors, from a major university. Everything about that experience had been grooming me for a PhD. Faculty cheered me on, fellow students affirmed me; even my best friend, with whom I had studied so hard, had been accepted into a doctoral program and was pursuing the academic dream. This was the expected path.

But as much as I love academia—let's be honest: I'm a total geek—a doctoral program is not the journey God has taken me on (or at least, not yet). Even before graduation, I sensed that I was to pursue writing again. That had been my vocation before graduate school, and many wise people continued to remind me about it. Meanwhile, I knew that eventually my husband would be appointed as the pastor of a church somewhere in Michigan; and unless we wanted to derail God's obvious call on his life, there was no point in applying to graduate programs in, say, New Jersey. So we put the academic thing on hold indefinitely and moved into a suburban parsonage in southern Michigan, and I resumed writing.

I'll admit: it was strange not to register for classes, come fall. As my friend described her professors and syllabi for the doctoral program, I couldn't help feeling envious. Every once in a while I'd wonder if I had missed the signs, misread God's plan. But then again, the thought of *not* writing, *not* helping my husband pursue God's call, *not* settling into ministry in our new setting—that didn't feel right either. And then we got pregnant, at which point the whole future became a roller coaster of unknowns.

So I can't claim to have this whole vocation thing figured out. Not even the mommy part. At one point in my life all the stars lined up for a career in academia, but then the planets shifted. If I had put all my dreams and hopes in that one direction, I would have been crushed. Even once we got pregnant there were no guarantees: Baby Arthur and even Mommy could have had a much harder road, and it was hard enough.

But once I started the journey, there was no use pining for some other life that I might have had, some other dream that supposedly slipped through my fingers. Motherhood is a worthy vocation, one that God has blessed. It is a gift, as the writer of Ecclesiastes 2:24 says: it is work in which a person can find great satisfaction. God has chosen this path for me—a path that many women all over the world, throughout history, have longed for—and it is my amazing privilege to walk it. And to be honest, I can't imagine it any other way.

-74-

Barefoot, Pregnant, and in the Kitchen?

I saw that there is nothing better for
people than to be happy in their work.
That is why we are here!

ECCLESIASTES 3:22

PREGNANCY FOUND ME in the kitchen. A lot. I had learned how to cook only the year before (my husband was the family chef), so I was a little slow. And I had gotten on this kick of making everything from scratch, which meant most recipes took forever. But often I was in the kitchen because I was hungry. Okay, really hungry. Like I could carve up a buffalo and sit down and eat the whole thing before my husband got home.

One afternoon I was peeling potatoes, listening to the radio, when the newscaster interviewed a woman who had just won a Nobel Prize. She spoke about her work, how she got started in the sciences back in the day when women were discouraged from such things. At one point she said,

"Most men I knew thought that a woman's place was barefoot, pregnant, and in the kitchen." And without thinking, I looked down at my feet.

Here I was, having recently received a master's degree, trying to finish a full-length manuscript, and I still had to pause and make sure I didn't fit the old stereotype. I looked down at my feet—or rather, leaned forward to look over my belly in the direction of my feet—and said out loud, "At least I have shoes on." Which I did, but only because I had stepped into the garage a moment earlier to take out the recycling.

Her comment smarted. I think I even left the dishes in the sink, went to my computer, pulled up an old paper from graduate school, and tried to read it. (*Tried* being the operative word here. Even today I pull out those old papers and think, *I haven't the foggiest idea what this woman is talking about.*) It bothered me all day. Was that all I had become? An old stereotype?

It would have been easy in that moment to start feeling bitter and resentful, wondering if I was wasting a perfectly good intellect by somehow reversing all the advances made by women over the past fifty years. But I had to remind myself that I was home because I *work* at home; I was carrying a baby because I felt *called* to; I was in the kitchen because I had *chosen* to learn how to cook; and I usually was barefoot because the dress code at my job is whatever I want it to be. There was nothing about my condition that had been forced on me.

But the grass is always greener, you know? Maybe that's why the author of Ecclesiastes repeatedly reminds us to take joy in our work (see today's Scripture). I thank God for the prizewinning chemists, I really do. I don't want their job. I don't even want to be writing papers for graduate school. When I pause and think about what I want, it's to be right here, holding my baby. This is work too!

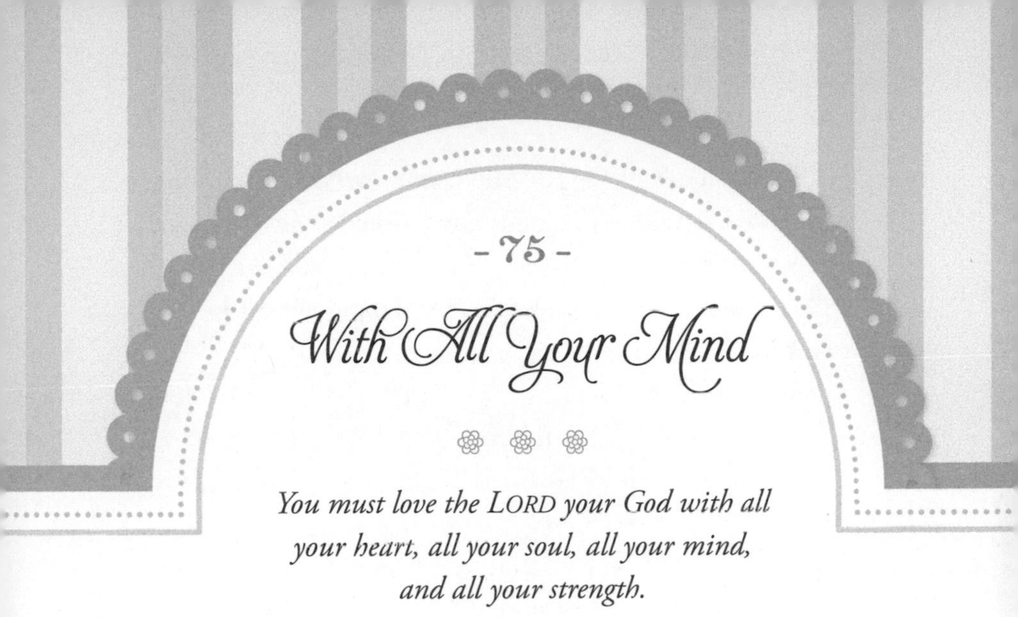

-75-

With All Your Mind

You must love the LORD your God with all your heart, all your soul, all your mind, and all your strength.

MARK 12:30

JUST WHEN I WAS BEGINNING to feel like pregnancy was the last nail in the coffin of my career as a writer (much less my almost career as an academic)—a chance encounter with a grocery-store clerk changed everything.

There was nothing special about the day or the store or the weather. I came in tired and grumpy, seven months pregnant but looking like I could pop at any moment. A woman in her early twenties, probably a student at the nearby university, began ringing up my purchases. As most people did at that stage in my pregnancy, she asked, "When are you due?"

"December fifteenth," I replied without enthusiasm.

She gave me a quick glance. "I'm sorry: I bet you get asked that a lot."

"Yeah. It's okay. I do have other things going on in my life, but this is pretty important."

"Like, what other things?" She seemed genuinely curious.

Surprised, I said, "Well, since you asked, I just finished writing a book."

She paused, a bag of carrots in her hand. "Seriously? For publication?"

"Yep."

"That's so cool! What's it about?"

Fumbling for words, I replied, "Um, it's a daily guide to prayer and stuff."

Now, generally when I describe the books I write, people have one of two responses: they either mutter something inane and change the subject, or their eyes light up and they tell me they're a Christian too. They never, ever say what this young woman said to me, which was the last thing I expected from a twentysomething at the local food co-op.

"Oh, are you a theologian?"

I was totally taken aback. If our town had a seminary, the word "theologian" *might* be common vocabulary around here. But even in seminaries I don't think theologians ask other theologians if they are theologians. Where the word came from in this girl's background, I have no idea. I wish now that I had asked her.

Instead I said in a startled voice, "Actually, I am. I studied theology in graduate school, and I write and speak about theological issues in youth ministry."

"No kidding!" she said. "That's so cool."

The customer behind me cleared his throat, signaling that the conversation had just wandered into awkwardness. I paid for my purchases and left the store.

But I left the store lighter, feeling like someone was helping me carry my extra forty pounds. All the anxiety and discouragement about my vocations, and how they might or might not mesh with mommyhood, had evaporated with that one simple question: Are you a theologian? Why, yes, yes I am, thank you. Seven months pregnant and all. The biggest, baddest, roundest, most hormonally freaked out theologian ever.

The mere fact that she asked the question was an affirmation. It felt like God's way of saying, "See? You are more than just a body, more than just a medical situation. You have a brain, and I'm going to keep using it for my glory. Just honor me." My child was going to grow up with a writer-theologian for a mother, one who takes the Bible seriously when it says to "love the LORD your God with . . . all your *mind*." And that was absolutely okay.

-76-

Productivity

On the seventh day God had finished his work of creation, so he rested from all his work.

GENESIS 2:2

THE JOKE IN OUR HOUSEHOLD is that my husband gets more done with his pinky finger in ten minutes than I do all day. And we're only partly joking. Tom has this amazing ability to multitask, rarely pausing for downtime; whereas I borrow much from the contemplative strand in my paternal DNA. The story goes that my great-grandfather, when his future son-in-law approached him about marrying his daughter, said, "You know that Lucille is very . . . *deliberate*." This was a kind way of saying, "It's not my fault if she drives you insane taking her sweet time with the silliest tasks. You've been warned."

My maiden name is Faulman, which means "lazy man" in German—and I suppose to the average person who has been schooled in a Protestant work ethic, that's an apt description. Although, if you know my father's family, there aren't many slackers among us. Dreamers, maybe. Artists. Hobbyists. People who have the amazing ability to putter around, doing what appears to be nothing. But we do it with great focus and determination.

Needless to say, when someone with my natural tendencies tries to live with someone like my husband—who manages to run all his errands in twenty minutes—it can be something of a train wreck. We have learned to adjust. A common question from my husband is "What were you up to today?" to which I often respond, "Um . . ." Over the years I have learned not to feel guilty (after all, in the past decade I have published eight books, earned a master's degree, learned to cook, drafted a novel, and had a baby); and over the years he has learned not to judge. We have grown in grace.

This was never more evident than in my first trimester of pregnancy. When he would ask, "What were you up to today?" I'd respond, "Well, let's see: I ate, and then slept, and then ate some more, then did some dishes, and fell asleep again. And then I woke up a few minutes ago and started working on dinner." One afternoon I didn't actually wake up from a coma-nap—which had begun after I cleaned up from lunch—until Tom was walking through the door, expecting dinner. Frustrated with my growing body, my unending appetite, the everlasting pile of dishes, my sheer exhaustion, I wailed, "I don't feel like I'm doing *anything*!"

The good man came over and hugged me. "You are producing *life*. I can't even imagine how much energy that takes. Go easy on yourself."

Those were the best words I could have heard in that

moment—words of grace. They reminded me that even God, after creating the universe and all living things, took the equivalent of a divine nap (see today's Scripture). Taking care of this infant, now that he's finally here, is work. Forget the laundry; forget my list of five billion other things to do. I am, with God, producing and sustaining *life*!

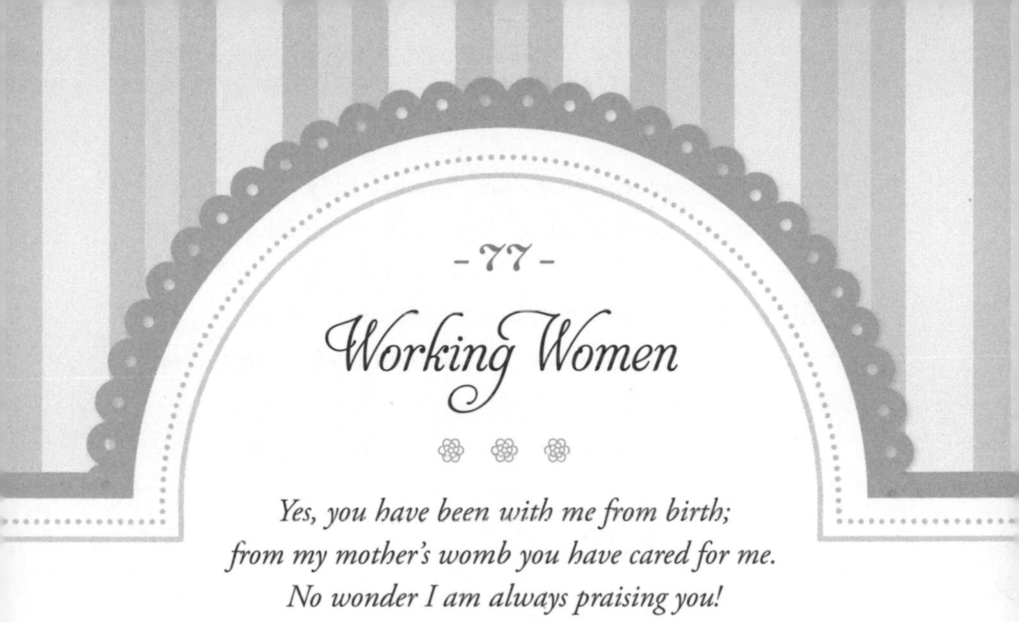

- 77 -

Working Women

Yes, you have been with me from birth;
from my mother's womb you have cared for me.
No wonder I am always praising you!

PSALM 71:6

THIS MORNING A FRIEND of mine posted online, "Sometimes I wish I was still pregnant so I could be with Will all the time." After giving birth to her son a few months ago, she has recently gone back to work. And, as she'll tell you, it's killing her.

After being with this child nonstop—both while he was in the womb and after he was born—for a year, she cannot shake the grief that seizes her every time she climbs in her car and drives away. Arms ache, mind strays, unreasonable panic overwhelms her. Guilt, like a slave driver, haunts her. She cannot remember, for the life of her, why work was ever so all-fired important.

But work she must, or the mortgage won't be paid. She and her husband will never get out from under college loans. And—perhaps more importantly—her hospice patients and their families, for whom she works so hard, will not receive the loving care they need. She's one of the lucky ones, she realizes. She not only has a job in the first place, but she has one that *matters*. But that doesn't lessen the tearing she feels when she puts her son in the arms of someone else and says good-bye for the day.

Many people like to think of the "good old days" when moms didn't have to work outside the home. Their husband's income was enough to support the family, and the women themselves could be with their children every moment, finish those household tasks that overwhelm the rest of us, even pick up a hobby or two. And I suppose on one level that was the case—for a brief window of time, for women of a certain class. But for the rest of the world, women have been working for other people, inside and outside of the home, for millennia or more.

Servants, midwives, doulas, nannies, nursemaids, governesses, cooks, scullery maids, sharecroppers, serfs, slaves . . . it all depends on which social class is yours by birth. In places like India, if you are born into the lowest caste, you might even be a prostitute or someone's personal slave against your will. Should you happen to get pregnant, your child belongs to your owner. The less power you have, the more likely you work for someone else, from birth to the grave.

Even here, the American Dream is quickly vanishing for our generation. We aren't slaves, but most of us work for someone else, in some form or other, in jobs that take us from home and children. And if we're not working, many of us are trying to find a job, or figuring out some way to work at home—which, believe me, is not as glamorous as it sounds.

If only all of motherhood was one big maternity leave! Instead we spend our first few weeks in a kind of sleep-deprived dream, gradually climbing up and out in time to start panicking about child care. Our brief time with baby slips away far too fast. But we can claim the promise that if God has been with our children, as the psalmist says, "from birth," then he will go with our children into whatever arms we must place them next.

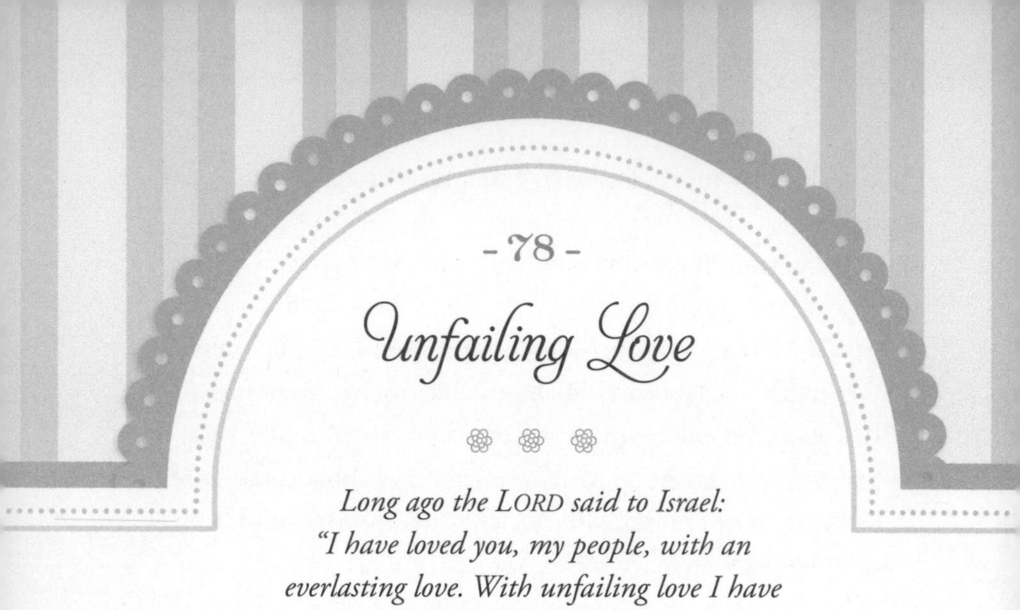

- 78 -

Unfailing Love

Long ago the LORD said to Israel:
"I have loved you, my people, with an everlasting love. With unfailing love I have drawn you to myself."

JEREMIAH 31:3

LONG BEFORE MICAH WAS BORN, I had agreed to speak at a winter youth retreat scheduled for this past weekend. At the time I thought, *Oh, no problem. By that point the baby will be a few months old, and my parents can help my husband, and it will be good for me to keep my career afloat. Plus, I will want to have a life by then.*

Right.

Last week, facing the retreat on the calendar, I began a kind of emotional meltdown. Twenty-four hours away from my son. Not just going back to work for a half day or for eight hours, but overnight. Not just dropping him off somewhere within driving distance, but taking off on a two-hour drive without him, on icy back roads, to some wintry cabin. Pumping milk alone in my cold room, hoping I had left enough for him, and then trying to act all happy and energetic among total strangers.

Maternity leave was over with a vengeance, and I hadn't even started packing yet.

Moms who work outside the home know exactly what I'm talking about. Long before your weeks are up, you're starting the panicked countdown, wondering how many emotional hits you can take before you fall apart completely. No one can read your child's cues like you can. No one can ease the ache in your own arms like your child can. The commute, the cubicle, the ring of well-wishing coworkers welcoming you back: none of it seems worthy of your sacrifice.

Until we have a baby, we have no idea what working parents go through. We think we'll be able to juggle it all, that we'll go on in life much the same as we did before this squirming bundle of needs and delights was handed to us. We know the first few months will be hard, but then, we assume, life will smooth out and we'll get back to "normal" (whatever that means). Ah, silly us. Crazy is the new normal. And crazy in love with our children is what we'll be, forever and ever, amen.

I can't help thinking about God as a heavenly Parent in this mode. Usually I envision God creating the universe, crafting human beings, and then going on with his usual business much as he did before. But what if giving "birth" to us rocked his world as much as having children has rocked ours? Yes, God is unchanging, the eternal Rock on which we stand. But he is also bound to us in unfailing love, as today's Scripture says. He longs for us to be with him, as a mother longs for her child.

What if this tearing we feel as working mothers, facing the inevitable separation, is only a small taste of what God feels when we wander away from him?

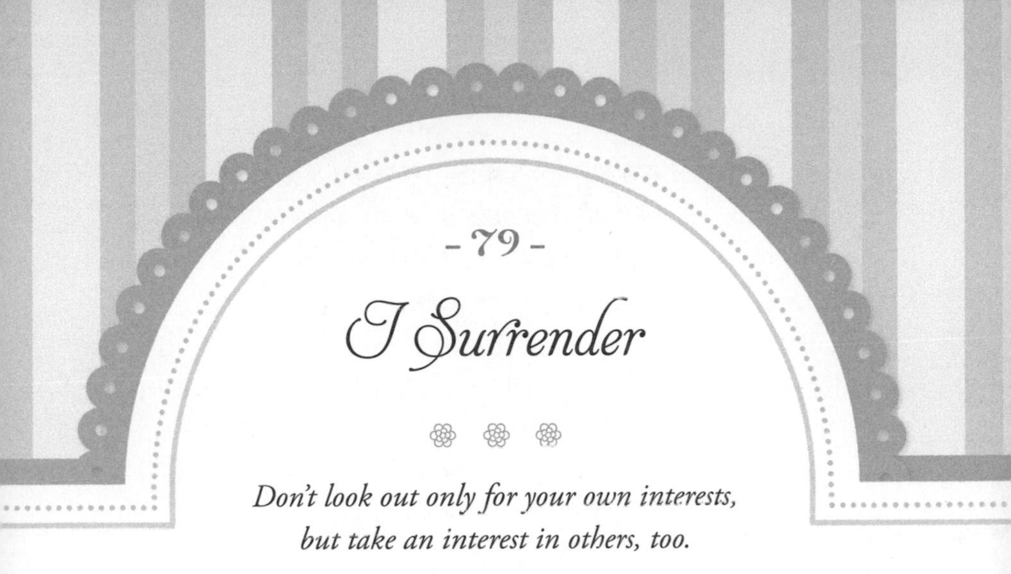

- 79 -

I Surrender

Don't look out only for your own interests,
but take an interest in others, too.

PHILIPPIANS 2:4

REMEMBER THOSE ELEMENTARY SCHOOL wrestling matches that ended with one or the other combatant hollering, "Say, 'Mercy'! Say, 'Mercy'!"? The loser whimpered or outright wailed, "Mercy!" and the winner let go. Surrender was not pretty, but someone had to do it.

That's my life at the moment. I want to win the wrestling match for sleep, but my crying child emerges the victor. I want to choose when and where we'll stop for a feeding, but I lose. I want to win the contest for whether we leave the house on time, but nope: another diaper blowout, and my baby grinning up at me on the changing table as if taunting, "Nana, nana, boo-boo." Baby: One. Mommy: Zero. I surrender.

If there was any risk of my becoming more self-obsessed at this stage in my life, all of that has been taken care of quite nicely by becoming a mother. Even if I wanted to obsess about myself, I have a tiny reminder (wailing, much of the time) that I am not the center of the universe. "We need reminding," writes Debra Rienstra in *Great with Child*, "and this is especially true in our self-indulgent culture, that if we foolishly imagine for a minute that parenthood is an accomplishment or achievement or right, sooner or later something will smack us with the realization that it is, above all, a surrender."[1] Someone is crying, "Mercy," and it's not my child.

Baby can't win all the time. (Not that you can spoil a newborn: forget what the old wives say. It's like saying you can spoil an unborn child in the womb.) Give me a few more months and I'll start pushing for him to participate in the whole family, not just his own little agenda. Hopefully I'll win some of the matches. Or maybe we'll become a team, helping each other—although that seems nearly impossible to imagine, while he is still so small and dependent. In any case, motherhood is a daily lesson in giving up my desires, in putting my own wishes aside for the moment and (as today's Scripture says) attending to the needs of another.

Such surrender is a spiritual discipline. It's a spiritual vocation, if you will. Rienstra puts it this way: "The giving over of my tiny helm is a chance to drift on something larger than myself."[2] Through this experience I'm learning not only that the world is bigger than my own needs and desires, but that God has an agenda larger than anything I can imagine. The ocean of his plan is vast, and thanks to motherhood, I have given up any illusions that I can always sail my own ship in the direction I want to go. Each day is a school for training my desires.

Thankfully, we can still cry, "Mercy!" And God hears us.

- 80 -

Saved through Childbearing?

Women will be saved through childbearing, assuming they continue to live in faith, love, holiness, and modesty.

1 TIMOTHY 2:15

SOMETIMES THE BIBLE seems so heavily masculine that I don't feel like I can find my footing. The apostle Paul, in particular, seems to have found himself speaking to churches that had an overabundance of silly women who wouldn't stop talking, so he felt the need to shut them down (see 1 Timothy 2:11-14, for instance). On one level, after surviving junior high, I can't say I blame him. Even just the other day my friend and I were writing at a coffeehouse (yes, writers have writing dates), and we overheard a small group of women from a local church complaining about some other woman who wasn't there. Any attempt by the leader to steer the conversation in a different direction was deftly ignored by the chief whiners, who grabbed the wheel and yanked the conversation back.

For an hour and a half.

At first I found the situation somewhat amusing, then irritating, then downright alarming. What would someone have thought who had rarely interacted before with Christians?

So perhaps Paul is justified in putting a check on such scenarios—although I don't know that gender needs to be the filter for discerning who gets the smackdown and why. But where things get really messy and uncomfortable is when Paul says something like today's Scripture: "Women will be saved through childbearing" (1 Timothy 2:15). And my first response is, "What the . . . ?"

Are women some sort of special class of animal, requiring a different spiritual program? Are women so bad, thanks to Eve (see 1 Timothy 2:14), that not even Jesus can save us? And what about those women who never bear children? Are they somehow not saved? In short, does this man have even the slightest clue what he's talking about?

Well, to be fair to ancient Greek (the language in which the New Testament was written), we readers aren't always sure we have the slightest clue what he's talking about. Some scholars insist that the presence of the definite article—which in English is *the*—means that the sentence should read, "Women shall be saved through the childbearing (or the child bearer)," a reference, perhaps, to Mary the mother of Jesus. Not that Mary saves us, but her willingness to reverse Eve's choice by submitting to the will of God played a significant role in everyone's salvation. Other scholars suggest that the phrase could read, "Women will be saved by the birth of the Child"—a reference to Jesus himself;[1] but that's not what ends up in many English translations, which in itself gives me pause.

In any case, the first part of 1 Timothy 2:15 comes linked to the second part, which reads, "Assuming they [women] continue to live in faith, love, holiness, and modesty." In other words, there's a caveat. Whatever else childbearing does for me, it's an opportunity for spiritual growth—if I'm willing. Salvation is a process, a continued quest to become more and more like Jesus. Any discipline that can make us holier—including fasting or celibacy or marriage or raising children—can be part of the process. But it doesn't matter how many children I bear if I don't continue to live in faith, love, and all the rest.

If it's not about Jesus, then I'm no holier than anyone else.

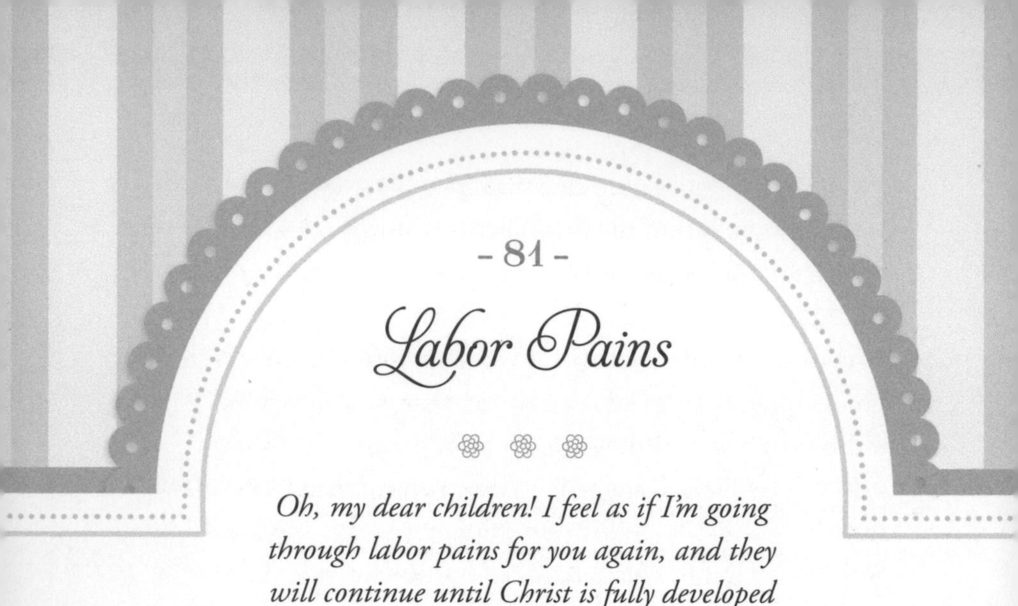

- 81 -

Labor Pains

Oh, my dear children! I feel as if I'm going through labor pains for you again, and they will continue until Christ is fully developed in your lives.

GALATIANS 4:19

I'VE ALREADY MENTIONED some of the more difficult biblical passages about women, particularly 1 Timothy 2:15 (see the previous devo, "Saved through Childbearing?"). But occasionally the biblical writers whip out a feminine image or reference that makes me feel at home. There are the wonderful midwives in Exodus 1, for instance, who hoodwink Pharaoh; and there's Isaiah 66:13, when God promises to comfort Israel like a mother—not to mention the numerous women and mothers, like Hannah in 1 Samuel 1, who seek to honor God. Even Paul, who often seems to be on the grumpy end of the biblical spectrum when it comes to women, makes use of feminine metaphors when trying to describe the life of faith.

Today's passage is one of those: a poignant and eloquent

expression of Paul's deep desire for the Christians in Galatia to mature. As one of the first Christian missionaries to plant churches around the Mediterranean, Paul helped convert thousands of pagans and Jews to Christianity. The new converts would begin meeting for worship and fellowship while Paul trained a team of leaders for that new congregation; and then he would move on to a different city. That's why most of the New Testament is made up of letters: Paul and the other Christian leaders maintained correspondence with the baby churches—encouraging, training, challenging, and occasionally disciplining.

Paul knew that just because you confess Jesus as Lord, it doesn't mean the journey is over. Yes, your sins are forgiven and you are, in Paul's words, a "new creation" (see 2 Corinthians 5:17, NRSV, and Galatians 6:15). But now comes the hard work of overcoming a lifetime of sinful habits—ways of thinking, ways of speaking, ways of acting. The goal, ultimately, is to become more and more like Jesus every day. Over time, people no longer see the old you—selfish, manipulative, greedy—but they see Jesus shining through you.

That's why Paul is concerned for the believers in Galatia. He worked so hard converting them and building the new church that he felt like a mother, giving birth in pain to something extraordinary. But now, a number of years later, he is hearing reports that the Galatians are going astray, deceived by false teaching, falling back into their old ways (see Galatians 1:6-7). All that hard work seemingly for nothing! But Paul didn't give up on the Galatians in the beginning, and he certainly isn't going to give up on them now.

He is like a mother all over again, breaking his heart in labor. He won't give up until Christ is "fully developed" in them.

Any mother who has gone through labor remembers how hard it is: we went through it once with our first child and the thought of going through it again is not exactly thrilling. But it's not just our task to bring this child into the world: we are charged with his or her spiritual formation as well (see Deuteronomy 6:6-7). It's like going into labor all over again.

As my son grows up and journeys in the life of faith, I have no illusions that *that* labor will be any easier than the first one. Lord, have mercy.

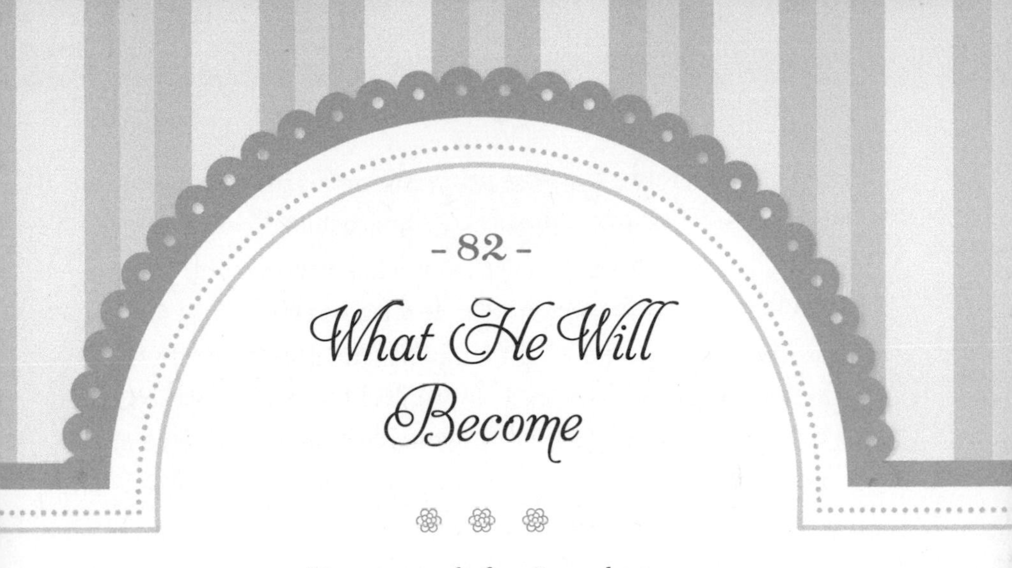

- 82 -
What He Will Become

You saw me before I was born.
Every day of my life was recorded in your book.
Every moment was laid out
before a single day had passed.
PSALM 139:16

IT'S HARD TO BELIEVE that at such a tiny age, my son's personality is already emerging. I'm not usually the one to spot it, actually: whatever he does just seems like normal baby stuff to me. But when I bring him to church asleep in his car seat, and he wakes up and starts fussing, and the fussing turns to crying and kicking, and his face gets all red, then the older women chuckle and say, "Oooh, he's mad! You've got a strong-willed boy there, Momma." And then I look at another infant who is crying and realize she sounds more like she has been deeply, deeply betrayed—a long, sad wail instead of the angry holler—and I think, *Great: I've got the tantrum child.*

The same thing happens at the doctor's office when I'm seeing a specialist. I'm up on the table while Micah hangs out in his car seat on the floor, but he can only handle that arrangement for so long before he starts to holler and turn red. But we're in the middle of the exam, and I can't do anything about it. We hear a thump from the car seat, where Micah has started kicking, and the specialist says, admiringly, "That was a solid kick." Another tantrum, and we haven't even had his three-month checkup yet.

Then we host the second reunion with our birth class friends. The babies are chilling throughout dinner, snuggled with a parent or settled in a swing or swaddled in a Moses basket—all except Micah, of course. My husband and I pass him back and forth, trying every possible trick to keep him from fussing and crabbing and complaining. Tom actually eats dinner bouncing on an exercise ball with Micah in the carrier on his chest, and even then Micah doesn't really settle down. After everyone leaves, Tom turns to me and says, "We have a fussy child." Yep. Now we know. This angry fussiness is not just babyhood: it's partly Micah.

All of which makes me worry: what sort of person will he become? I envision a strong-willed bellyacher who kicks things when he's mad. The vision is not comforting. Those are the kinds of kids I've always sworn my children will never be, having assumed that nurture plays a stronger role than nature in such scenarios. The last thing I want is for my son to spend his entire childhood in time-out. But if he gets angry so easily, we'll have our work cut out for us. Just thinking about the whole thing makes me tired.

God has known all this ahead of time, of course. As today's Scripture says, God knows each day of Micah's life before it has even passed. Micah still has the free will to make his own choices, but God has the ultimate oversight. I can only pray that someday God will use Micah's strong will to his glory, helping Micah take a stand against injustice, for instance. And I can pray that in the meantime I'll be given a measure of God's own strength and creativity to face the difficult days with God's own love.

- 83 -

Real Love

This is real love—not that we loved God, but that he loved us and sent his Son as a sacrifice to take away our sins.

1 JOHN 4:10

AS IT TURNS OUT, my son's angry fussiness is not just his emerging personality (see the previous devo, "What He Will Become"). The fact is, he probably doesn't feel good. Or so his doctor thinks, and I'm inclined to agree. Yes, he is a sensitive kid, prone to getting mad quickly. But he has good days and bad days, and we're beginning to wonder if they're sometimes linked to what I'm eating. Whatever I consume passes to him eventually, and while I've been cautious about some of the foods that can temporarily produce colic in nursing babies (cabbage, for instance), I haven't held back on eating whatever I want.

"So, what do I do?" I ask my doctor.

"Well, you need to eliminate the most likely suspects first and then reintroduce them slowly."

"Such as . . ."

"Dairy, eggs, shellfish, nuts, chocolate, wheat . . ." The list goes on.

There is a pause. Just the implications of "no dairy" alone are taking up all my mental energy. Wait. No cheese? No butter? No yogurt? Adding up all the other off-limit foods, my brain quickly scans my usual recipes and ditches them, one by one.

"Is there anything left that I *can* eat?" I finally say.

My doctor grins. "Good luck."

And so it begins. The Save the Baby Weird Diet Challenge is under way. I stand by the fridge, staring longingly at my favorite Greek yogurt, and turn my back with a sigh. I won't even open the freezer for a last glimpse of Death by Chocolate ice cream. It will take a few weeks before all of these foods are out of my system, at which point I can start to reintroduce them one by one. I'm counting down the days. *The things we do for our children . . .*, I think to myself, with a martyred shake of my head.

At first I can manage it. What's a few weeks? But within ten days, Micah's fussiness has dropped significantly. Even the tantrums have eased up. I think back to his worst days and realize, "Oh, yeah, I had that huge plate of baked French toast that morning." He still kicks and turns red when he's upset, but he reaches that threshold less quickly and less frequently. So, rather than take a gamble and reintroduce those food items into my diet again, and spend more days in Fussy Baby Purgatory, I decide to go cold turkey.

Yep. That's it. It's not just a temporary diet, but a complete change in eating habits for the rest of the foreseeable future.

As long as Micah is nursing—which I hope will be at least another year—I will be the annoying one at restaurants who asks if the rolls are made with real butter or if there are dairy-free dessert options. Rather than torture myself, I throw away the ice cream. *The things we do for our children . . . ,* I think to myself. And this time I'm just plain mad.

I want to be able to do this gracefully. I want to be the kind of parent who can make sacrifices for her children with a smile, gently shrugging her shoulders and saying, "Ah, but it's all worth it!" But honestly, if I meet that parent right now, I might smack her. And maybe she doesn't exist. Maybe the only parent who doesn't tally the cost, who gives it all up out of pure love (as today's Scripture says) is God. *Lord, whatever you've got, I need some.*

- 84 -

When Your Children Ask

We will use these stones to build a memorial.
In the future your children will ask you,
"What do these stones mean?"

JOSHUA 4:6

I'VE BEGUN COLLECTING a box of mementos from these first few months of Micah's life. Ultrasound pictures, paperwork from the hospital, cards from friends and family, his tiny footprints. Someday, I tell myself, I will put them all in a scrapbook. Micah and I will go through it when he is older, oohing and aahing over his cuteness; and of course he'll be deeply interested, wanting to know all the stories about when he was tiny and if he really pooped fifty-six times a day.

Given my past attempts at scrapbooking, this vision is highly unlikely. The stuff will most likely stay jumbled in a box until Micah graduates from high school, at which point I'll go through it again, sighing and crying, unable to part with any of it. And meanwhile, if Micah is anything like my friend Jami's boys, once he's older he'll be mostly interested in the ultrasound pictures because they make him look like a Freddy Krueger Alien Pirate Skeletor, which is really cool.

Of course, our whole house at the moment is a memento of this season in our lives. We have artifacts for helping him sleep: everything from cradles to cribs to swings to baby carriers to strollers. We have standing monuments to feeding the baby, including stacks of burp rags within ten feet of any spot in the house. In time, most of these things will be stored or given away, to be replaced by toys and tricycles and other shrines to toddlerhood. If and when we ever move, we'll have to drag it all out; and Micah will say, "What's that?" and we'll launch the whole story about how this was a special kind of baby carrier that required a degree in origami to figure out.

What will not be as obvious from this time in his life is the spiritual journey his parents have been on. There aren't as many natural mementos for that sort of experience. Sure, we might keep track of some of our prayers and challenges, insights and questions, in letters or e-mails or journal entries, but overall we don't leave monuments around the house that prompt a spiritual story. Now I'm wondering if maybe we should.

It was a common practice for the Israelites, after all. Often, when something significant happened, they were commanded to build an altar or practice a ceremony or make a pile of stones as a memorial.[1] That way, in future years, when their children asked what those things meant (as in today's Scripture from Joshua 4), the parents were to tell the story of how God had delivered them. And it wasn't just a suggestion: they were *commanded.* "When your children ask in time to come," the parents were told, ". . . then you shall tell them . . ."[2] The "shall" is key: it's a directive. Storytelling is a commandment.

So what if we kept mementos from our spiritual journey around the house, prompting questions? (I'll discuss this a bit more in the following devo.) Then someday, when Micah asks what these things mean, we can respond to God's command by telling the stories that actually matter.

- 85 -

God in the Everyday

You must commit yourselves wholeheartedly to these commands that I am giving you today. Repeat them again and again to your children. Talk about them when you are at home and when you are on the road, when you are going to bed and when you are getting up.

DEUTERONOMY 6:6-7

WHAT MEMENTOS of our family's spiritual journey do I want to have around for Micah to ask questions about someday? I began mulling over this question in the previous devo, but now I wonder if I'm splitting hairs a bit too much. I mean, it's hard to separate your spiritual life from the rest of what you do—not to mention, much of this devotional book has been about finding God in the everyday mess, in the mundane tasks of motherhood. God is not somehow aloof from the material world: he is there in the dailiness, intimately involved in my son's small universe of eating, sleeping, snuggling, and pooping.

I'm reminded of a seventeenth-century monk named

Brother Lawrence, who was known for practicing the presence of God in the midst of everyday life. Because he didn't have an education, when he entered the monastery he was assigned to one of the lowest positions, working in the kitchens. Monasteries often fed hundreds of brothers as well as guests, so the kitchens were regularly scenes of chaos. But Brother Lawrence, in the middle of the mess, humbly cultivated a sense of God's presence while doing simple tasks. Lawrence didn't limit prayer to the brief moments he spent in the chapel: he could turn a pancake for the love of God. He could wash a pile of pots and pans, viewing each one as a different brother in need of prayer. Mundane tasks became vehicles for communing with Christ.

Moses encouraged a similar approach when schooling the Israelites in how to best follow God's commandments (see today's Scripture). Don't do them just in those moments or places that seem uniquely "spiritual," but when you're waking up in the morning, or taking the usual commute, or dropping your kids off at day care. Talk about them with your kids over and over, till the stories and commands are as familiar as the family histories that get told around the table at Thanksgiving. Because *this is your life*, this story God is telling through you. It's not a separate spiritual narrative, told in a special spiritual voice, saved for special spiritual occasions. It's right now.

So maybe it's not so much that I fill the house with religious kitsch, but that everyday items become monuments to God's presence in our lives. When Micah is older and we pull out all the stuff from his infancy that we've stored in the basement, and he asks, "Mommy, what is this?" maybe my response can be more than just, "It's a complicated baby carrier." Maybe I can say, "It's a complicated baby carrier that I used to keep you close to me when you were tiny. Just like our heavenly Father keeps us close and never lets us go, I held you near my heart."

(Of course, by that time he'll probably say, "Ew!" and run away from my attempts to hug him, but let's not think about that yet. . . .)

- 86 -

Never Too Early

Future generations will hear about the wonders of the Lord.
His righteous acts will be told to those not yet born.
They will hear about everything he has done.

PSALM 22:30-31

THERE'S A SERIES of pictures featuring my mother holding Micah when he is just days old, reading to him *The Tale of Peter Rabbit*. In one picture he's studying her face; in another he seems to be engrossed in the story. No doubt at this age he's merely attracted by the sound of her voice, the movement of her hands turning the pages, the colors and shapes in the book, the stripes of her shirt. He has no more idea of bunnies and gardens and men with rakes than you or I have of life on Mars.

But, my mother insists, it's never too early to start reading with him. I do it even now, a few months later, in my half-crazed attempts to establish a "bedtime routine." Sometimes I feel absolutely ridiculous, narrating the eating habits of a ravenous caterpillar to an infant who does nothing but stare and drool and occasionally yawn. But every once in a while I sense a stirring, the lift of an eyebrow, his breath coming a little more quickly or released in a long sigh, as the caterpillar turns into a butterfly.

Perhaps it's my imagination; perhaps there's nothing more going on than the comfort of mommy-baby time. Whatever the case, I am passing along something I feel is important for his sense of being: his participation in a world and a story larger than himself. Even if the horizon is limited for now to caterpillars and to bunnies that say good-night to everything in the room, Micah is learning that stories are important—that stories, like food, are vital to life.

Our faith comes to us through the best story of all, the story of God in Christ. Among the pile of board books by the rocker are the Jesus books: the stories of Jesus blessing the children or feeding five thousand people with food donated by a boy. In time Micah will know that the Jesus stories are tied to what we pray before meals, and what happens when we go to the place called church, and when Mommy's friends come over with their Bibles. He will begin to link the words of the Lord's Prayer, which we say every night, with the stories of the Prodigal Son ("forgive us our debts") and the Transfiguration ("for thine is the kingdom, and the power, and the glory"[1]) and all the great tales we find in God's Word. It's more than just a legacy of reading we want to pass along, but a way of life shaped by the book that matters most.

It's never too early to start. As the psalmist says in today's Scripture, God's "righteous acts will be told to those not yet born." No doubt that line is simply meant to reiterate the idea that future generations will hear about God. But I like the other image it conjures too: that of a pregnant mother talking away to her unborn child, telling him or her about all the great things God has done. If it can start that early, then surely it can start now.

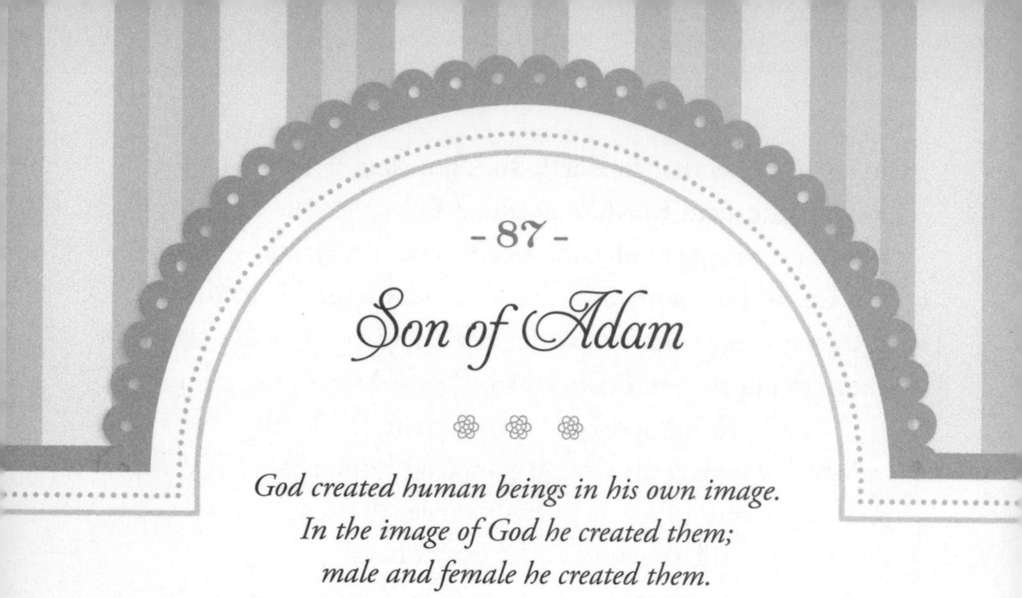

- 87 -

Son of Adam

God created human beings in his own image.
In the image of God he created them;
male and female he created them.

GENESIS 1:27

I'M ALREADY SCHEMING about the stories I will read to Micah as he gets older, stories I hope he will return to on his own. Top of the list? The series the Chronicles of Narnia, by C. S. Lewis. Rich with allusions to faith, the Chronicles have the potential to smuggle in more truth through his imagination than I could ever do through mere talking.

In one of my favorite scenes, from the book *Prince Caspian*, a young human prince learns from the lion-king, Aslan, that he is descended from pirates. Disappointed, Prince Caspian admits, "I was wishing that I came of a more honorable lineage." Aslan replies, "You come of the Lord Adam and the Lady Eve, and that is both honor enough to erect the head of the poorest beggar, and shame enough to bow the shoulders of the greatest emperor on earth. Be content."[1]

Through Aslan's statement, Lewis is alluding to the

biblical notion that human beings are creatures of tremendous dignity and worth, descended from the first humans, made in the image of God (see today's Scripture). Adam and Eve walked with God and were made caretakers of all creation—they were, as I've already noted, not much lower than the angels (see Psalm 8; see "Mere Mortals," pp. 24–26). In addition, God became incarnate in the form of a human through Jesus Christ, honoring humanity with the greatest dignity of all. It is this knowledge, Lewis suggests, that should raise the head of the lowest beggar.

But as descendants of Adam and Eve, humans also inherit their shame. Our ancestors broke God's law by eating fruit from the forbidden tree (see Genesis 3), and the guilt of their trespass is handed down from generation to generation through our spiritual DNA, you might say, only to be cleared by the death and resurrection of Jesus Christ. We can never escape from that heritage except through the faith of Christ, in whom we are "new creations" (see 2 Corinthians 5:17, NRSV). It is this knowledge that should bring humility to the highest person of prestige and power.

I hope that Lewis's notion of human dignity and shame will be both an encouragement and a caution to my son as a young reader. As tough as it may be for me to admit, someday he may think he can never overcome a painful memory or persistent sin and become the person God has called him to be. *Prince Caspian* can encourage him to claim his true heritage as a son of Adam, descendant of the first human steward of creation, made in God's image. But if he is more like me (true confessions, here), someday he may fall into the opposite sin of spiritual pride, thinking he is on a level above the sinning populace. To be reminded of his shameful spiritual ancestry—which he shares with everyone else—could be an important corrective toward proper spiritual humility.

All this scheming before he can focus his eyes on the page, much less read. . . . But I can hope, can't I?

- 88 -

From Generation to Generation

Each generation should set its hope anew on God,
not forgetting his glorious miracles
and obeying his commands.

PSALM 78:7

MY NINETY-NINE-YEAR-OLD grandfather is dying. We have known this for some time, ever since Grandma passed away last spring. He has hung on, holding out for his one-hundredth birthday and the anniversary of her going.

Grandma didn't live long enough to meet Micah. But after the visitation, while everyone else was chatting in the front porch of the funeral home, I slipped back to where she lay and whispered to her that I was pregnant. Other than my sister and cousin, she was the first of our family who I told. I don't know that she heard me in any traditional sense of the word: it was more symbolic than anything. But it was important to me.

And now her widower is dying. It takes us a good three

hours to reach his nursing home, but we make the trip through the snow, determined that Micah will spend even a little time with him. Aware of Grandpa's failing health and of time slipping away so quickly, I hand Micah to him with a mixture of joy and grief. This is a beloved man, someone I've cherished and admired since my first days of life. And he has cherished and admired his grandchildren, lavishing thoughtful words and gestures on us from the beginning. Rare in his generation, he says out loud what he is feeling, how much he loves us, how much he hopes we will follow Jesus.

So I hand Micah to him and say, "Grandpa, is there anything you want to say to Micah? Anything you'd like him to know?"

"Oh yes," he says, his voice weak and trembling. His hands are confident with my son's small body—he has held his share of babies in a century; only his voice shakes. "I want you to know that we love you. I want you to know that Jesus loves you. There's nothing greater than following him all your life." His voice nearly vanishes with the effort. But he has said what he wants to say. Now he just gazes at the baby, taking in Micah's various expressions, studying his tiny thumb.

My mother captures the moment in an amazing photo: my son's tiny, flawless fingers grasping my grandfather's ancient, veined, and bony hand. A century between them. All the things my grandfather has witnessed in a lifetime, all the technological advances, the kingdoms that have risen and fallen . . . my son has touched it briefly. My son will one day say with astonishment that he was held in the arms of a man who, in his childhood, had known Civil War veterans. And all of that history is a treasure.

But none of it compares to the words my grandfather has shared in this moment. The legacy of faith he has passed on to Micah is not a thing of the ancient past, but a promise of the future, a calling, a chance to bear witness to the eternal story. It is an opportunity, as today's psalm says, for Micah to set his hope on God. My prayer is that Micah and his great-grandfather will meet again one day; and Micah will be able to say, "You were right. There has been nothing greater than following Jesus all my life."

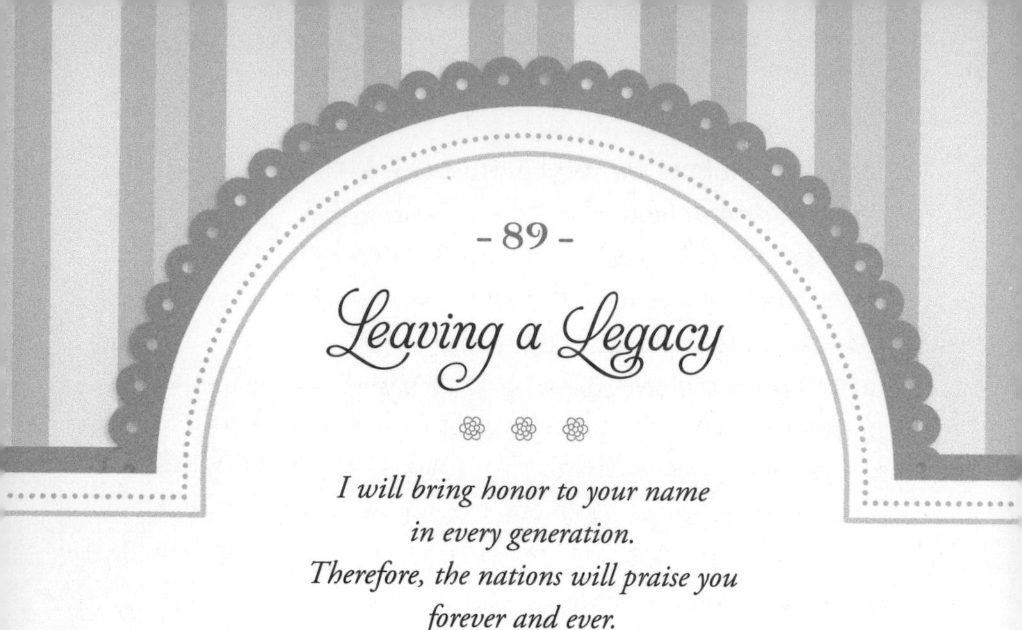

- 89 -

Leaving a Legacy

I will bring honor to your name
in every generation.
Therefore, the nations will praise you
forever and ever.

PSALM 45:17

MICAH WILL NOT REMEMBER his great-grandfather the way I do (see the previous devo, "From Generation to Generation"). He probably won't remember him at all—unless there is some dim, untapped reservoir of infant memories that rests latent in us, surfacing every now and then in odd dreams or déjà vu. He'll see pictures of him, of course; and I'll tell stories. I'll remind him of the words that his great-grandfather shared with him when he was tiny, the encouragement to walk with Jesus all his days. And I hope that Micah will live out those words, that he will think of his great-grandfather and the rest of the loving adults in his life when faced with decisions. I hope he'll choose those things that would honor my grandfather's prayers for him.

Especially when Micah hits those teenage years. When the vast, complex, graceless world opens up to him, offering so many avenues for error and vice, I will pray that he'll remember who (and whose) he is. It's not that I don't want him to take risks: because he will. It's that I'll want him to take risks for Jesus: to make his own way against the pulse of the crowd; to stand against injustice; to love mercy; to walk, as his forebears have sought to walk, humbly with his God (see Micah 6:8).

But more than that: I will pray that he thinks of his own great-great-great-grandchildren. As I've suggested to many a teenager in my youth ministry work, it's not just about looking behind you, to see who's watching and taking names. It's not about whether or not the choice you're about to make will get you in trouble with the grown-ups in your life. It's also about looking ahead, considering how this choice will affect the people who come after you. What legacy are you leaving? What memory will your children's children pass along to their own kids? How will you be remembered by those who you will never meet but who bear your name and your legacy, for better or worse?

As Christian music artist Sara Groves says in her song "Generations," those who come after us will reap what we sow. After sorrowing that the choice of Eve was so damaging to those who came after her, Sara recognizes that she herself can pass on "a curse or a blessing" to those she will never know. And then in a line that always slays me, Sara sings, "To my great-great-great-granddaughter: live in peace."

Live in peace. That's the prayer. By what I do today—by the choices I make in this hour, this moment—may my descendants experience the peace of God. This is the legacy

I want to leave, the kind that my grandfather is giving to us. Not a legacy of wealth or influence; not one of heirloom junk or endless collectibles; but a spiritual legacy of peace, in which we set our descendants up for being a blessing rather than a burden in the world.

When Micah is older, I'll invite him to write a letter. He'll pull out some nice, manly stationery, or maybe type on a tablet the size of his thumb, and address it "To my great-great-great-grandson."

I wonder what he'll say.

- 90 -

I Remember

O LORD, what are human beings
that you should notice them,
mere mortals that you should think about them?
For they are like a breath of air;
their days are like a passing shadow.

PSALM 144:3-4

SO, MY SON HAS LOST that wrinkled, alien look. His body is firming up, his cheeks are rounder, his thighs are chunky with rolls of fat. We moved up to the next size of diapers long ago. Unfortunately, all that beautiful newborn hair rubbed off in stages—there was a stretch when he looked like my grandfather, sporting the same pattern of baldness he will no doubt revisit in sixty-odd years. Now he's just plain bald, like a cue ball, and sturdy enough to roll.

I'm trying not to grieve the changes—for pity's sake, the child is barely three months old! But it's hard not to think with a sigh of his newborn stage, of those teeny newborn clothes, the little bitty diapers (true confessions: I saved one—a *clean* one). I fold one of his receiving blankets, now used as a burp rag, and can hardly believe we used to swaddle him in it. Where have these three months gone?

Of course, in the middle of things each day feels like forever. Older moms keep telling me to treasure each moment because time passes so quickly. I stare at them with the incredulity of a POW. Really? Would you trade places with me? Because (especially when I'm nursing or my son is fussy) there are some days that can't pass quickly enough. I can hear every tick of the clock, watch every angle of the sun as it slants slowly across the room. Um, what shall we do now? Ah yes, transfer the wash to the dryer. Done. Watch the snow falling, falling, forever and ever, amen. Feed the baby. Chop some celery. Wait for Daddy to come home. Where *is* the man, anyway?

And yet here we are, crossing the three-month mark, and I have no idea where the time has gone. I'm the type of person who's prone to nostalgia, and yet motherhood doesn't allow many opportunities to wallow in it. I suppose there will be plenty of time for that when he's older and out of the house, making his own way in the world. I will be like those old ladies at the grocery store who, when they see Micah, smile sadly and shake their heads and say things like, "I remember when mine were that small." They reach for him, then, and touch his little foot, as if all that intimacy and affection are a distant dream.

I remember. Someday that will be my line too. I don't know that I'll want to relive these three months. I doubt it. But I will remember the weight of his little body in my arms, the soft breaths when he sleeps, the way his eyes watch me move around a room. I will remember that I was his whole world, and he, in so many ways, was mine. All of it will have passed, as the psalmist says, like a breath of air, like a shadow. But God will have met us here in the strange country that is Mommy Time. And I am grateful.

ABOUT THE AUTHOR

SARAH ARTHUR is the author of numerous devotionals on the spiritual life, including *The One Year Coffee with God: 365 Devotions to Perk Up Your Day*. A fun-loving speaker for women's retreats, conferences, and events, she encourages women to seek God in the midst of the ordinary. When she isn't chasing her toddler, Micah John, around the house, she can be found blogging at www.saraharthur.com and twittering @HolyDreaming. She and her family live in Lansing, Michigan.

Interested in having Sarah speak at your women's event? E-mail assistant@saraharthur.com.

Also by Sarah Arthur

In a warm, casual, conversational style, Sarah Arthur takes you on a transformational journey. One day at a time, she explores both the subtle and the startling ways God shows up in our lives.

HAVE A CUP OF COFFEE AND CONNECT WITH GOD.

Find more devotions at www.tyndale.com.

CP0643

MORE RESOURCES FOR MOMMY TIME

Sarah Arthur, *The One Year Coffee with God: 365 Devotions to Perk Up Your Day* (Carol Stream, IL: Tyndale, 2011).

Amy Gaither Hayes, *A Collection of Wednesdays: Creating a Whole from the Parts* (Grand Rapids, MI: Zondervan, 2011).

Sarah Jobe, *Creating with God: The Holy Confusing Blessedness of Pregnancy* (Brewster, MA: Paraclete Press, 2011).

Debra Rienstra, *Great with Child: On Becoming a Mother* (La Porte, IN: WordFarm, 2008).

David Robinson, *The Busy Family's Guide to Spirituality: Practical Lessons for Modern Living from the Monastic Tradition* (New York: Crossroad Publishing Company, 2009).

Gary Thomas, *Sacred Parenting: How Raising Children Shapes Our Souls* (Grand Rapids, MI: Zondervan, 2005).

Gary Thomas, *Devotions for Sacred Parenting: A Year of Weekly Devotions for Parents* (Grand Rapids, MI: Zondervan, 2005).

SCRIPTURE INDEX

NOTES

MERE MORTALS

1. For example, see the King James Version.

THE WISDOM OF HUMILITY

1. See Harvey Karp, *The Happiest Baby on the Block* (New York: Bantam, 2002).

CALM IN THE STORM

1. C. S. Lewis, *Mere Christianity* (New York: HarperOne, 2001), 198.

MATTER *MATTERS*

1. Debra Rienstra, *Great with Child: On Becoming a Mother* (La Porte, IN: WordFarm, 2008), 27.

GOD'S COMPASSION

1. *Rechem*, according to *Strong's Concordance*.

THE LONG GOOD-BYE

1. Excerpted from Kathleen Norris, "Ascension," in *Little Girls in Church* (Pittsburgh: University of Pittsburgh Press, 1995), 42.

HERE TO SERVE

1. One Greek lexicon gives the meaning of *doulos* as "attendant," one who is "devoted to another to the disregard of one's own interests."
2. For example, see Matthew 21:33-39 and Luke 14:16-24.
3. For example, see 2 Corinthians 4:5; Philippians 1:1; and Titus 1:1 (all NKJV).

SELF-EMPTYING

1. Earlier I discussed this same verse in the devo "The Form of a Doula" (pp. 143–145) using a different translation and exploring a different theme. Amazing how rich God's Word is!

UNCLEAN?

1. See Leviticus 12.
2. See, for instance, the instructions for becoming ceremonially clean from a skin disease, as found in Leviticus 14:1-32.
3. See Leviticus 15:19-24.

TRUE FAMILY

1. Tertullian, "The Passion of the Holy Martyrs Perpetua and Felicitas" in *Ante-Nicene Fathers*, ed. Philip Schaff, vol. 3, Christian Classics Ethereal Library, http://www.ccel.org/ccel/schaff/anf03.vi.vi.iii.html.

CROWD OF WITNESSES

1. Paraphrased from Tertullian, "The Passion of the Holy Martyrs Perpetua and Felicitas" in *Ante-Nicene Fathers*, ed. Philip Schaff, vol. 3, Christian Classics Ethereal Library, http://www.ccel.org/ccel/schaff/anf03.vi.vi.vii.html.

I SURRENDER

1. Debra Rienstra, *Great with Child: On Becoming a Mother* (La Porte, IN: WordFarm, 2008), 41.
2. Ibid., 10.

SAVED THROUGH CHILDBEARING?

1. See footnote on 1 Timothy 2:15 in the New Living Translation.

WHEN YOUR CHILDREN ASK

1. See, for example, Exodus 12:26-27; Deuteronomy 6:20-25; and Joshua 4:4-7.
2. See Joshua 4:6-7, NRSV.

NEVER TOO EARLY

1. Wording from the King James Version.

SON OF ADAM

1. C. S. Lewis, *Prince Caspian: The Return to Narnia* (New York: HarperCollins, 1951), 218.